Title:
The Brazilian Tax Reform
Format: Digital and Print Book
Distribution: Print and Digital
1st Revised Edition
Copyright © Heron Robledo – 2024

ISBN: 978-65-01-15758-0

Heron Robledo

THE BRAZILIAN TAX REFORM

Bill 68/2024

A Practical Guide to Mastering the New Rules

CONTENTS

INTRODUCTION.

Since the early 1960s, the Brazilian tax system has undergone significant changes, reflecting the needs of a constantly developing country. The tax system, which was initially simple and focused on a few taxes, has become increasingly complex with the emergence of new taxes and contributions over the decades. Each tax brought with it specificities that increased the bureaucratic burden and ancillary obligations for taxpayers. The history of some of the main taxes is crucial to understanding the current scenario and the urgency of the Tax Reform proposed by Bill No. 68/2024.

ICMS-Tax on the Circulation of Goods and Services.

The ICMS was established by the 1988 Federal Constitution, replacing the former Tax on the Circulation of Goods (ICM), created in 1967 during the Tax Reform promoted by the military government. The main function of ICMS has always been to allow states and the Federal District to collect taxes on the circulation of goods and certain services, such as transportation and communication. Over the years, the ICMS has become the largest source of revenue for the states, but it has also generated great complexity due to the different rates applied among federal entities, leading to the so-called "fiscal war" between states.

ICMS Rate History.

ICMS rates vary from state to state, with the initial rate defined by the 1988 Constitution. Initially, the general rate was around 17% for most states. However, over time, states adjusted the rates according to their fiscal and economic needs, leading to significant variations. The so-called "fiscal war" intensified with the granting of tax benefits, creating competition among states to attract companies, which generated greater discrepancies in rates. Currently, rates can vary between 12% and 25%, depending on the state and the type of goods or services.

IPI-Tax on Industrialized Products.

Created by the 1967 Constitution, the IPI is a federal tax levied on industrialized products. Its regulatory function allows the federal government to use the tax as an economic policy tool, adjusting rates to stimulate or curb production in certain sectors. Since its creation, the IPI has been used as an industrial incentive tool, but it has also become a significant tax in federal revenue, being calculated based on the added value at each stage of industrialization.

IPI Rate History.

The IPI has a regulatory characteristic, meaning its rates can be adjusted by the federal government according to economic and fiscal objectives. Historically, rates have varied between 10% and 20% for most industrialized products. However, products considered essential or strategic, such as basic food items, have reduced rates or exemptions. Luxury products, such as high-value cars, alcoholic beverages, and cigarettes, have always had higher rates, often exceeding 30%. The government has also used the IPI as a tool to stimulate national industry, temporarily reducing rates for strategic sectors during times of economic crisis.

ISS-Service Tax.

The ISS was established by Decree-Law No. 406 of 1968 as a response to the growing demand from municipalities for their own source of revenue. It is a municipal tax levied on the provision of services. Over the years, the ISS has been expanded to cover a broader range of services, reflecting the economic changes in Brazil, such as the growth of the service sector in the economy. However, like other Brazilian taxes, the ISS has faced challenges related to rate uniformity and taxation in different municipalities.

ISS Rate History.

The ISS also varies according to the municipality, but Complementary Law No. 116 of 2003 established a minimum rate of 2% and a maximum rate of 5% for the tax. Historically, rates tended to be closer to the lower limit (2%) for services with higher demand elasticity, such as technology and advertising. However, as service provision gained more relevance in the economy, many cities began applying higher rates, especially for luxury services or specific professions, such as law and consulting.

PIS-Social Integration Program.

The PIS was created in 1970 during the military government as a social contribution aimed at financing unemployment insurance and other social integration policies. Its tax base is the gross revenue of companies, and over the decades, the PIS has undergone several reforms, including the establishment of PIS/PASEP, and more recently, its convergence with COFINS under the non-cumulative regime for certain companies.

PIS Rate History.

PIS rates vary depending on the tax regime. In the cumulative regime, the historical rate has always been 0.65% on gross revenue. With the introduction of the non-cumulative regime by Law No. 10,637 of 2002, the rate was increased to 1.65%, allowing companies to take credit for acquired inputs. These changes were made to make the tax fairer and avoid cascading taxation, but they also introduced greater complexity into the system.

COFINS-Contribution for the Financing of Social Security.

COFINS was established by Complementary Law No. 70 of 1991 with the aim of financing social security, including health, welfare, and social assistance. Like PIS, COFINS is levied on companies' gross revenue, and over time, it was also adapted to the non-cumulative regime, which introduced complexity in the calculation and assessment of this tax for companies. COFINS has become one of the main sources of funding for Brazil's social security system.

COFINS Rate History.

Like PIS, COFINS also has differentiated rates between the cumulative and non-cumulative regimes. In the cumulative regime, the rate has always been 3%, but with the creation of the non-cumulative regime by Law No. 10,833 of 2003, the rate was increased to 7.6%. COFINS has become one of the most impactful taxes for companies, especially due to its incidence on gross revenue, without any distinction between profit margins or sectors.

CSLL-Social Contribution on Net Profit.

Created by Law No. 7,689 of 1988, the CSLL is a social contribution levied on the net profit of companies, aimed at financing social security. The CSLL was designed as a way to ensure that companies contribute directly to the financing of social policies, complementing the revenues obtained by the Union through traditional taxes.

CSLL Rate History.

CSLL was initially created with a rate of 8%, applied to the net profit of companies. However, over the years, the federal government made several adjustments to this rate, with specific increases for certain sectors. In 1997, the rate was reduced to 9%, a value that remains to this day. In sectors such as finance, the rate has been raised several times, reaching 20% on some occasions as a way to increase revenue and distribute the tax burden more equitably.

IRPJ-Corporate Income Tax.

IRPJ is one of the oldest and most important taxes in the Brazilian tax system, dating back to the 1920s. However, its modern structure was defined over the years, with significant reforms in the 1960s and 1980s. IRPJ is levied on companies' profits and has different assessment regimes, such as actual profit, presumed profit, or arbitrated profit, which provides flexibility for companies but also increases complexity in tax planning.

IRPJ Rate History.

IRPJ has undergone several changes over the decades. Until the early 1980s, the effective IRPJ rate was significantly lower than it is today, ranging between 10% and 20%, depending on the sector. Since 1995, the rate has been set at 15% on assessed profits, with an additional 10% for profits above a certain threshold. This additional charge aimed to increase revenue from large companies, but it also increased the complexity of tax calculation, as different tax brackets were created for IRPJ.

The Evolution to Bill 68/2024.

Over the decades, the overlapping of taxes, lack of simplification, and fiscal competition between states and municipalities have created a tax system that is widely considered one of the most complex in the world. Several attempts at reform have been made over the years, but none have been able to solve the system's main problems, such as the high tax burden, excessive bureaucracy, and federative disputes.

Bill No. 68/2024 proposes a radical change in this scenario, unifying taxes and simplifying the tax collection process. The proposal aims to create a Goods and Services Tax (IBS), which would replace ICMS, ISS, IPI, PIS, and COFINS, providing a fairer, more modern, and efficient system. This book will examine this reform in detail and its potential impacts on Brazil, both economically and socially.

Comparison between the Current Tax System and Bill 68/2024.

The Brazilian tax system, marked by a diversity of taxes and contributions, has evolved over the decades with the creation of taxes such as ICMS, IPI, ISS, PIS, COFINS, CSLL, and IRPJ. These changes reflected the economic needs of each period but also made the system increasingly complex and burdensome. Bill 68/2024 proposes a break with this model, aiming to simplify the tax structure through the creation of a Goods and Services Tax (IBS), which unifies various taxes and adopts a more modern rate system.

ICMS vs. IBS.

ICMS stands out for its complexity due to varying interstate and intramunicipal rates, as well as the "fiscal war" between states. Currently, rates vary from 12% to 25%, depending on the state and type of goods or services, which creates distortions in the system. Bill 68/2024 proposes replacing ICMS with IBS (Goods and Services Tax), which will have a single rate for each federal entity, promoting greater simplicity and eliminating disputes between states. By unifying rates, the goal is to create a more competitive and efficient business environment.

IPI vs. CBS.

IPI, historically used as an industrial and economic policy tool, has rates that range from 10% to over 30%, depending on the product. Bill 68/2024 absorbs IPI into CBS, eliminating regulatory specificities and standardizing taxation on industrialized products. This change aims to simplify tax incidence, reducing the bureaucratic burden for companies, while seeking to boost the competitiveness of national industry without the need for frequent rate adjustments.

ISS vs. IBS.

ISS, a municipal tax, will also be integrated into IBS. Today, ISS rates range from 2% to 5%, depending on the service and municipality, which creates difficulties for companies operating in multiple cities. Bill 68/2024 proposes a single rate system for services, eliminating the multiplicity of local rules and standardizing collection at the national level. This measure aims to facilitate the lives of service companies and reduce fiscal fragmentation.

PIS and COFINS vs. CBS.

PIS and COFINS have been sources of complexity for companies, especially after the adoption of the non-cumulative regime, with rates of 1.65% for PIS and 7.6% for COFINS. These contributions generate a series of complex assessments, with the right to credits on inputs and operations. With the creation of CBS, Bill 68/2024 unifies PIS and COFINS, simplifying taxation and eliminating cumulatively, providing fairer and less bureaucratic revenue collection.

CSLL and IRPJ.

CSLL and IRPJ, although not directly incorporated into IBS, will also undergo significant adjustments in the context of tax reform. Bill 68/2024 maintains IRPJ and CSLL separately but simplifies the calculation process, eliminating complexities and providing a single rate on company profits. The proposed rates for IRPJ must be reviewed, especially the additional 10% on profits above a threshold, with the aim of reducing production costs and promoting greater competitiveness for the Brazilian business sector.

Rate Evolution in Bill 68/2024.

While the current system presents a wide variation in rates between different taxes, Bill 68/2024 proposes a radical simplification, with the creation of single rates for CBS and IBS for each federal entity (Union, states, and municipalities). In addition, the bill provides for the gradual elimination of tax cumulatively, reducing the tax burden on production chains and encouraging economic growth. The central idea is that CBS will have a neutral rate, calculated to avoid increasing the total tax burden but instead redistributing it more equitably.

The text approved by the Chamber of Deputies does not define what can be called the maximum rate for CBS and IBS, that is, the rate to be charged from sectors not benefiting from exemptions. Both taxes will be instituted by complementary law. The CBS (federal) rate can be set by ordinary law. However, since the government cannot afford to lose revenue, the maximum rate, estimated at 26.5% (8.8% for CBS and 17.7% for IBS), would compensate for the exceptions provided in the proposed constitutional amendment (PEC).

What is VAT.

VAT (Value-Added Tax) is a broad-based tax, widely adopted in various countries around the world, which is levied on the added value at each stage of the production and commercialization chain of goods and services. In other words, it is applied to the value added to the product or service at each phase of its manufacturing, distribution, and commercialization. One of the main objectives of VAT is to avoid the cumulative effect of taxes, meaning that a tax is not charged multiple times throughout the production chain, creating a "cascading effect." This tax aims to replace multiple indirect taxes, simplifying the tax system and promoting greater economic efficiency.

Functionality.

VAT operates on a non-cumulative basis. This means that, at each stage of production or service provision, the tax is calculated based on the added value, not on the total value of the good or service. Each company along the production chain can credit the tax paid in previous stages, paying tax only on the value it has added to the product or service.

For example, a car manufacturer pays VAT on the parts it purchases but can deduct this amount from the VAT it charges when selling the finished car.

The final consumer is the only one who bears the full VAT amount, as they cannot deduct the tax.

Maximum VAT Rate.

The VAT rate varies between countries, and in Brazil, with the possible adoption of VAT under Bill 68/2024, the rates are expected to be adjusted according to the type of product or service. In general terms, the maximum VAT rate in Brazil, according to recent discussions, will be 26.5%. This maximum rate is projected to tax higher-value or less essential goods and services, such as luxury products, automobiles, and appliances.

On the other hand, essential goods such as food, medicine, and basic services may be taxed at a reduced rate, or even exempt from VAT, depending on the political and economic decisions made by the government and the National Congress.

This variation in rates aims to ensure that the tax is progressive, avoiding an excessive burden on the most vulnerable classes and ensuring that basic necessities remain accessible to all.

VAT Implementation Timeline in Brazil.

The VAT implementation timeline proposed by Bill 68/2024 is gradual, recognizing the complexity of the current tax system and the need for adaptation by both taxpayers and tax administrations. The transition to the new system is expected to take place over a period of five to eight years, with progressive stages of implementation.

First Phase (Years 1 to 2):

In the first stage, the Goods and Services Tax (IBS) will be created and regulated, replacing taxes such as ICMS, ISS, PIS, COFINS, and IPI. During this phase, VAT will be applied in parallel with the old taxes, allowing for a smoother transition for taxpayers and tax authorities.

Second Phase (Years 3 to 5):

As the system becomes more adapted, the old taxes will progressively be phased out. ICMS and ISS rates will gradually be reduced, while IBS/VAT will take on a more prominent role. Companies and service providers will have already adapted their tax calculation systems to the new format.

Third Phase (Years 6 to 8):

In this final stage, IBS will be fully operational, replacing the previous indirect taxes. ICMS, ISS, PIS, COFINS, and IPI will be officially abolished, and operations will follow exclusively the VAT calculation model. The focus will be on consolidating the new system, with adjustments made to correct any inefficiencies or issues identified throughout the process.

During the implementation timeline, the federal government may also adjust rates and transition rules to avoid economic shocks and maintain the competitiveness of the productive sector. Additionally, compensation measures will be provided for states and municipalities that may lose revenue during the transition.

Expected Benefits of VAT.

The adoption of VAT in Brazil, following the model proposed in Bill 68/2024, aims to simplify the tax system, increase transparency, and improve the competitiveness of Brazilian companies, which currently face a huge bureaucratic burden to meet their tax obligations. Moreover, the non-cumulative nature of VAT is expected to reduce companies' indirect costs and help combat tax evasion, as the credit system encourages the proper recording of transactions at all stages.

Another expected benefit is increased international competitiveness, as VAT is a model widely used in various countries, allowing for greater economic integration and facilitating foreign trade.

WHAT IS CBS.

CBS (Contribution on Goods and Services) is a new tax introduced with Bill 68/2024, a tax reform proposal in Brazil. Its primary goal is to simplify and unify the consumption tax system by replacing three federal taxes: PIS (Social Integration Program), COFINS (Contribution for Social Security Financing), and IPI (Tax on Industrialized Products). CBS is a value-added contribution, with an approach similar to VAT (Value-Added Tax) adopted in many countries.

CBS will be applied at all stages of the production chain, from production to the commercialization of goods and services, allowing for the offsetting of tax credits along this chain. This means that companies will be able to deduct the amount of CBS paid on their input purchases from the amount due on their sales, avoiding tax cumulatively and promoting greater tax efficiency.

Rate Set by the Federal Government.

According to the government's economic team, the maximum projected VAT rate is 26.5%. The standard reference rate for CBS will be 8.8%, set by the federal government. This rate will be uniform across all sectors and economic activities, except for specific cases provided by law.

The definition of a single rate aims to simplify the tax system, reducing the distortions caused by the diversity of rates and regimes previously in place. The choice of the 8.8% rate reflects a balance between the need for revenue collection and the impact on prices and the competitiveness of goods and services.

Churches and Temples.

Regarding churches and religious temples, Bill 68/2024 maintains the tax immunity provided by the Federal Constitution for activities of an essentially religious nature. Therefore, strictly religious activities of these institutions will be exempt from CBS. However, commercial activities conducted by these entities, such as the sale of products or services, will be subject to CBS. This means that, although churches and temples are not taxed on their income from religious activities, they will need to pay CBS on the income obtained from their commercial operations, following the same logic applicable to other commercial entities.

Automotive Industry.

The automotive industry, a sector with significant economic and social relevance, will be significantly impacted by the introduction of VAT. The 8.8% CBS rate will be applied to vehicles and parts, replacing IPI, which is a specific tax on industrialized or equivalent products.

The implementation of CBS will bring changes to the tax structure of the sector, particularly regarding the offsetting of tax credits.

The automotive industry may benefit from the possibility of offsetting VAT credits throughout the production chain, which could help mitigate the impact of taxation on the final cost of vehicles. However, the impact of the new rate on the sector's competitiveness and the final product prices will still be a point of concern, especially considering that the automotive sector often benefits from state and federal tax incentives.

In summary, CBS will represent a significant change in the Brazilian tax system, aiming for greater simplicity and transparency. The single rate of 8.8% is one of the key features of the new tax, while its application to churches and temples only for commercial activities and its impact on the automotive industry will be crucial aspects for the adaptation and implementation of the tax reform proposed by Bill 68/2024.

WHAT IS THE IBS.

IBS (Goods and Services Tax) is a tax proposed by Bill 68/2024, aimed at replacing ICMS (Tax on the Circulation of Goods and Services) and ISS (Tax on Services of Any Kind). The goal of IBS is to simplify the state and municipal taxation system, promoting greater uniformity and transparency in consumption taxation in Brazil.

IBS is a value-added tax that applies to goods and services throughout the production chain, similar to the VAT model adopted in several countries. The introduction of IBS seeks to eliminate the disparities between state and municipal tax regimes, promoting a more coordinated and efficient approach to tax collection on consumption.

What is the rate?

The proposed IBS rate will be 17.7%. This rate will be uniformly applied to all transactions of goods and services, replacing the current ICMS and ISS, which have variable rates depending on the state or municipality. The single rate of 17.7% aims to simplify taxation, reducing the complexity and bureaucracy associated with the different rates and regimes currently in place.

Furthermore, the introduction of IBS will have a direct impact on state and municipal revenues, which were previously collected through ICMS and ISS. To compensate for potential losses in revenue, Bill 68/2024 provides for a resource redistribution mechanism that ensures adequate compensation for states and municipalities, ensuring the continued funding of local and regional public services.

Ecological IBS.

The concept of "Ecological IBS" is an innovation introduced by Bill 68/2024, aimed at promoting environmentally sustainable practices. The Ecological IBS provides tax benefits or incentives for companies and consumers who adopt sustainable practices and products. This could include a reduction in rates for goods and services that meet specific environmental criteria, such as low carbon emissions, the use of recyclable materials, or energy efficiency.

The implementation of Ecological IBS will be accompanied by a set of rules and regulations that will define the criteria for granting tax benefits and the monitoring mechanisms to ensure compliance with environmental standards.

Conclusion.

IBS, as established by Bill 68/2024, represents a significant restructuring of the Brazilian tax system, aiming to simplify and standardize the taxation of goods and services. The proposed rate of 17.7% is an initial reference, but the legislation allows states and municipalities to set the final rates.

According to Section VI of Bill 68/2024, the IBS rate will be determined by each federative entity. The federal government will set the CBS rate, while states and municipalities will have autonomy to define their own IBS rates. The Federal District, in turn, will exercise both state and municipal powers in setting its rates. This means that, despite the initial proposed rate of 17.7%, each state and municipality may adjust its IBS rate, either increasing or decreasing it relative to the reference rate.

Each federative entity may link its rate to the reference rate of the respective government level or set it independently. In the absence of specific legislation establishing a rate, the defined reference rate will apply. Furthermore, any changes to the IBS rate must comply with a 90-day waiting period, ensuring that adjustments are not applied immediately.

Therefore, while Bill 68/2024 sets a maximum reference rate for VAT, the flexibility given to states and municipalities in setting rates could result in significant variations in the effective rates applied. This will allow each federative entity to adjust its rate according to its specific fiscal and economic needs, promoting greater adaptability to local realities, but also creating a scenario of additional complexity that will require effective coordination between the different levels of government.

WHAT IS THE SELECTIVE TAX(IS).

The IS (Selective Tax) is a new tax proposed by Bill 68/2024 that aims to replace the current taxes on specific and selective products, such as the IPI (Tax on Industrialized Products) and other taxes that serve both regulatory and revenue-generating purposes. The IS will be a tax levied on specific goods and products, with the goal of regulating and discouraging the consumption of products considered harmful to health or the environment, or that have a significant impact on economic and social issues.

Unlike CBS and IBS, which are taxes on value-added and on goods and services, respectively, the IS is focused on the taxation of specific products, exercising a selective and regulatory function. This tax is intended to discourage the consumption of products whose production and use may have negative effects and to promote more effective public policy in areas of interest such as public health and environmental protection.

Which Products Will Be Taxed by IS.

Bill 68/2024 specifies that IS will be applied to a range of products that may include:

1. Luxury Goods: Products considered to be of high value or luxury, which may include high-displacement vehicles, jewelry, and high-cost items.

2. Health-Harmful Products: Products that pose significant public health risks, such as cigarettes, alcoholic beverages, and foods with high sugar, salt, or saturated fat content.

3. Environmentally Harmful Products: Products whose use or disposal can cause environmental damage, such as certain types of non-recyclable plastics, pesticides, and polluting chemicals.

4. High Energy-Intensity Products: Goods that consume large amounts of energy or natural resources in their production and use, such as large household appliances and industrial equipment.

The specific list of products that will be taxed under IS will be defined in additional regulations and may be adjusted over time according to political and social needs.

What are the IS Rates?

Bill 68/2024 establishes that IS rates will vary depending on the nature of the taxed product and its regulatory impact. IS rates are not fixed and can vary according to the product category and regulatory purpose. The bill specifies that the rates will be set to reflect the selective purpose of the tax:

1. Health-Harmful Products: For products such as cigarettes and alcoholic beverages, the rates tend to be higher to discourage consumption and promote public health. The rate for these products may be significantly higher than for less harmful products.

2. Luxury Goods: Luxury products will also be subject to elevated rates, reflecting their non-essential nature and the high purchasing power of consumers of these goods.

3. Environmentally Harmful Products: The rate for products that cause environmental harm will be adjusted to encourage a reduction in the use of such products and promote more sustainable alternatives.

4. High Energy-Intensity Products: For products that consume large amounts of energy, the rates may be adjusted to reflect the environmental cost associated with

their use and incentivize the adoption of more efficient technologies.

In summary, the IS is a selective tax designed to regulate and discourage the consumption of products that have negative impacts on health, the environment, or are considered luxury items. The rate setting will align the fiscal and regulatory goals of the tax, reflecting the social and economic impact of each product category. Variable rates and the list of taxed products will be detailed in additional regulations, ensuring that the IS effectively meets the public policy objectives established by Bill 68/2024.

WHAT IS THE COMPENSATION FUND.

The Compensation Fund is a mechanism established by Bill 68/2024 to ensure a smooth and balanced transition between the old and the new tax system. Its primary function is to compensate for potential revenue losses for states and municipalities that may occur during the implementation of the new IBS and IS rates, as well as to assist in adapting to the new tax model.

Objectives of the Compensation Fund.

1. Fiscal Balance. The fund aims to ensure that states and municipalities do not experience significant revenue losses during the transition period. As Bill 68/2024 changes the tax bases and rates, some federative entities may face a temporary reduction in revenue, particularly if the new tax structure results in an uneven redistribution of income.

2. Smooth Transition: The fund provides a financial buffer to help soften the economic impact of the reform, allowing federative entities to adjust to the new system without major financial disruptions. This is particularly important for states and municipalities that rely heavily on ICMS and ISS revenues.

3. Incentive for Adaptation: In addition to providing financial compensation, the fund also encourages a quick and efficient adaptation to the new tax system, ensuring that the change does not lead to economic instability.

How the Compensation Fund Works.

1. Fund Financing: The fund will be financed through a combination of resources, which may include contributions from the federal government, transfers of resources from CBS and IS revenue, and other sources of income provided by law.

2. Resource Distribution: The fund's resources will be distributed to states and municipalities based on criteria established by law, which may consider revenue loss, population size, and other economic and fiscal variables.

3. Compensation Period: Financial compensation will be adjusted over a defined period, providing gradual support as federative entities adapt to the new rates and the new tax structure.

Implementation Timeline.

The implementation of the Compensation Fund is set to begin upon the enactment of Bill 68/2024. According to the project, the fund will become operational from the date the new CBS and IBS rates are applied. The transition to the new system will occur gradually, with financial compensation being provided during a transitional period defined by law.

This transitional period is established to ensure that states and municipalities can adjust their budgets and fiscal systems without facing extreme financial difficulties. The exact timeline for the fund's implementation and the duration of the compensation period will be detailed in specific regulations and the transition schedule set by Bill 68/2024.

In summary, the Compensation Fund is a crucial mechanism in Bill 68/2024, designed to mitigate the financial impact of the tax reform on states and municipalities and ensure an orderly transition to the new system. The implementation timeline and operational details of the fund will be defined in additional regulations, but its creation is an important step toward ensuring fiscal stability during the implementation of the tax reform.

WHAT IS TAXATION ON SPECIFIC REGIMES.

Taxation on specific regimes, as defined in Bill 68/2024, refers to a set of rules and exceptions applied to certain sectors or types of taxpayers that, due to their special characteristics, do not fit perfectly into the general taxation regime established for CBS (Contribution on Goods and Services), IBS (Goods and Services Tax), and IS (Selective Tax). These regimes aim to address the economic and social particularities of certain sectors, ensuring that they are taxed fairly and appropriately, taking into account their relevance or specificities.

Main Features of Taxation on Specific Regimes.

1. Priority Sectors: Specific regimes are applied to sectors considered to be priorities or strategic for the country's economic and social development. This includes sectors with characteristics that justify the need for differentiated taxation, such as:

Agribusiness: Due to its importance for the economy and exports, differentiated regimes may be applied to ensure competitiveness.

Technology Industry: Sectors that promote innovation and development may benefit from specific tax incentives.

Education and Health: Private educational and healthcare institutions, which play a significant social role, may be covered by special tax regimes.

2. Micro and Small Businesses: Bill 68/2024 acknowledges the importance of micro and small businesses in Brazil's economic and social landscape. For these businesses, which operate with reduced profit margins and face significant challenges, there are provisions for simplified tax regimes, reducing the tax burden and associated bureaucracy.

3. Manaus Free Trade Zone and Free Trade Areas: The Manaus Free Trade Zone, for example, is a region with tax benefits that promote the development of the Amazon. Bill 68/2024 preserves these special regimes, allowing these regions to maintain their tax incentive characteristics to attract investment and create jobs.

4. Differentiated Regime for Exports: Taxation on specific regimes also applies to the export sector, which traditionally benefits from tax exemptions to ensure international competitiveness. Bill 68/2024 provides for the continuation of specific regimes for exports, with no CBS or IBS levied on products destined for foreign markets.

5. Churches and Religious Temples: Religious institutions have historically received differentiated tax treatment in Brazil, respecting the principle of religious freedom. Bill 68/2024 maintains this tax exemption, ensuring that churches and temples remain exempt from taxes like CBS and IBS, preserving their role in society.

Details of Specific Regimes in Bill 68/2024.

Bill 68/2024 details specific regimes in Title IV, which regulates differentiated treatment for sectors that require a special tax regime. Key details about these regimes include:

1. Reduced Rates: Certain sectors or activities may benefit from reduced rates, meaning taxes are charged at rates lower than those under the general regime. This applies to sectors the government considers strategic or of high social and economic importance, such as education, health, and even agribusiness.

2. Exemptions: Some sectors may be exempt from certain taxes, as in the case of exports or religious institutions. These exemptions ensure that exported products or religious activities are not directly impacted by taxes that could hinder their economic or social function.

3. Differentiated Regime for Technology and Innovation Industries: The bill includes provisions to encourage innovation, with special tax regimes for startups and technology companies, aiming to foster technological development and make Brazil more competitive globally.

4. Simplicity in Compliance with Tax Obligations: Micro and small businesses will benefit from simplified regimes, with simpler procedures for calculating and paying taxes. This is essential to reduce the bureaucracy these businesses face and facilitate their operation in the market.

5. Transition Period for Specific Sectors: Some sectors will have longer deadlines to adapt to the new CBS and IBS rules, as provided for in the legislation. This allows for a smoother transition, minimizing the immediate financial impact on these sectors.

Conclusion.

Taxation on specific regimes in Bill 68/2024 aims to adjust the tax system to the particularities of strategic and socially relevant sectors. With reduced rates, exemptions, and simplified procedures, the bill seeks to balance fiscal revenue collection with economic development. The maintenance of specific regimes is essential to ensure that vital sectors, such as education, health, innovation, and exports, continue to perform their roles without the tax burdens that could compromise their operation and competitiveness.

WHAT IS THE REGIONAL DEVELOPMENT FUND.

The Regional Development Fund (FDR) is one of the main innovations of Bill 68/2024, created with the goal of promoting economic growth and reducing inequalities among the different regions of Brazil. This fund aims to support balanced regional development, especially in historically less developed areas, such as the North and Northeast, ensuring that these regions have the financial and structural conditions to grow economically and compete with more developed regions like the Southeast and South.

The FDR represents an important fiscal and economic policy tool, extending beyond the simple collection of taxes. Its purpose is to ensure that the resources generated by the new tax system are distributed fairly and efficiently, promoting the development of regions with lower wealth generation capacity and that require strategic investments to become competitive.

Main Features of the Regional Development Fund.

1. Reduction of Regional Inequalities: The creation of the FDR acknowledges the need to address the economic and social disparities between different regions of Brazil. Historically, the country's economic

development has been concentrated in wealthier regions like the Southeast, while regions such as the North and Northeast have struggled to keep pace due to a lack of infrastructure, investment, and resources. The FDR aims to correct these inequalities by ensuring a more equitable distribution of resources.

2. Infrastructure Development: One of the main focuses of the FDR is financing infrastructure projects in less developed regions. This includes investments in areas such as:

- Transportation: Construction and improvement of highways, railroads, ports, and airports to enhance the flow of production and regional mobility.
- Sanitation: Expansion and improvement of water and sewage systems, which are essential for public health and quality of life.
- Energy: Investments in energy generation and distribution, particularly in renewable sources, to ensure adequate and sustainable supply in more remote areas.

3. Private Sector Incentives: The FDR also aims to encourage private investment in less developed regions. This could include the provision of subsidized loans or other tax incentives for companies that choose to set up factories or production units in these areas, stimulating job creation and local economic growth.

4. Integration with Regional Policies: The fund will be integrated with regional development policies, coordinated with state and municipal government initiatives. The goal is for FDR resources to be applied efficiently and in synergy with ongoing projects, maximizing the impact of investments.

Financing of the Regional Development Fund.

The financing of the Regional Development Fund (FDR) will come from various sources outlined in Bill 68/2024. The main source of revenue will be a portion of the funds collected from the IBS (Goods and Services Tax), ensuring that a portion of the revenue generated by this tax is dedicated exclusively to regional development. As IBS is gradually implemented, the fund will receive an increasing share of the resources generated.

In addition, the FDR will be supported by contributions from the federal government, specific funds, and partnerships with international financial institutions involved in financing development projects. These diverse sources of funding are critical to ensuring the fund's ability to invest in large-scale infrastructure and other strategic initiatives.

Management and Allocation of Resources.

Bill 68/2024 provides for the creation of a governance structure for the Regional Development Fund (FDR), which will be responsible for managing and overseeing the allocation of resources. This structure will be composed of representatives from the federal government, states, and municipalities, along with specialists in regional development and infrastructure.

FDR resources will be allocated based on technical criteria that prioritize projects with the greatest impact on regional development. This includes a cost-benefit analysis, socioeconomic impact, and project feasibility, ensuring that resources are allocated efficiently and strategically.

Implementation Deadlines and Conditions.

The implementation of the Regional Development Fund will be gradual, following the transition schedule of the new tax system outlined in Bill 68/2024. As IBS is implemented and resources begin to be collected, the FDR will also be progressively capitalized and operationalized.

It is expected that the fund will begin to be effectively financed in the early years after the IBS takes effect, with a portion of the collected revenues being redirected to the FDR. This schedule will be detailed in complementary regulations, which will define the percentages of resources the fund will receive at each stage of the new tax system's implementation.

Conclusion.

The Regional Development Fund is a central mechanism in Bill 68/2024 to ensure the equitable development of Brazil. It acknowledges the importance of addressing historical regional disparities, promoting sustainable economic growth and infrastructure improvements in less developed regions. With efficient management, the FDR will play a key role in the long-term strategy to strengthen the economies of areas that have been neglected in terms of investment and economic development. The fund will be essential in ensuring that the new tax system not only generates more revenue but also fosters a more just and balanced society.

What is the Managing Committee.

The Complementary Law Proposal (PL) 108/2024, also known as the Law for the Management and Administration of IBS (Goods and Services Tax), was approved by the Chamber of Deputies on August 23, 2024. It introduces new important rules and guidelines for Brazil's tax reform. The text is divided into several parts, or "books," addressing topics such as the management of IBS, the process of oversight, the distribution of collected resources, and issues related to other taxes like ITCMD (Inheritance and Donation Tax).

Administration and Management of IBS.

The IBS Managing Committee (CG-IBS) will be the body responsible for overseeing the coordination and management of IBS. This committee will include representatives from the states, municipalities, and the Federal District. Together, they will ensure that the new tax system operates smoothly and efficiently.

Functions of the IBS Managing Committee.

The Managing Committee will play a crucial role in making the tax reform work in practice. It will:

- Create rules and regulations for IBS.

Organize how the tax will be collected and audited.

- Distribute the money collected between states and municipalities fairly.

The committee will also coordinate the auditing and collection of IBS, bringing together the administrations of states and municipalities. In addition, it will be responsible for managing information technology systems, ensuring everything operates efficiently and securely.

Operational Guidelines.

The committee will be divided into several departments, each with a specific function. For example:

- Auditing Department: Will handle the auditing of IBS.

- Collection and Revenue Department: Will be responsible for managing the tax collection.

Another important aspect is technology governance. The Information Technology Department will be responsible for developing systems that facilitate the collection and auditing processes, increasing transparency and efficiency.

The goal is to ensure that resources are fairly allocated between states and municipalities. The committee will establish the distribution criteria, taking into account factors such as:

- Population.
- Level of economic development.
- Social needs of each region.

This distribution aims to promote fiscal balance between the different regions of Brazil, ensuring that all areas have access to the necessary resources for growth and development.

ITCMD and Other Provisions.

The second part of PL 108/2024 addresses the ITCMD (Inheritance and Donation Tax), which is the responsibility of the states and the Federal District. The proposal establishes how this tax will be administered and collected, as well as setting rules for exemptions and reductions. For instance, there will be an exemption from ITCMD for donations made to philanthropic or cultural projects, as a way to encourage such activities.

Procedural Rules.

PL 108/2024 proposes the modernization of the tax administrative process, making it faster and less bureaucratic. One of the main advancements is the use of electronic systems for submitting documents and resolving disputes. This will facilitate communication between different federative entities and reduce the time spent on bureaucratic procedures.

Additionally, a specific system will be created to resolve disputes related to IBS more efficiently, ensuring that decisions are fair and consistent.

Guidelines for Collection and Auditing.

The law also establishes clear rules for the collection and auditing of IBS. The Managing Committee will work in collaboration with the tax administrations of states and municipalities to ensure the proper collection of the tax and to conduct efficient auditing.

Distribution of IBS Revenue.

The revenue collected from IBS will be distributed according to criteria such as population size and the level of economic development of each state or municipality. Additionally, an adjustment will be made to the initial revenues to ensure that the funds are redistributed fairly over the years.

During the transition period, from 2029 to 2077, a portion of the revenue will be withheld and redistributed among the states and municipalities to accommodate the new distribution model.

Transparency and Oversight.

PL 108/2024 also introduces rules regarding the transparency and oversight of revenue collection. The Managing Committee will be responsible for publishing periodic reports showing how resources are being collected and distributed. This is essential to ensure that the process is fair and transparent.

Next Steps.

After the presentation of PL 108/2024, the next steps are:

1. Discussion in congressional committees.
2. Public hearings.
3. Approval by the committees.
4. Voting in the Chamber of Deputies.
5. Senate proceedings.
6. Presidential approval.
7. Regulation and implementation of the changes.
8. Preparation for the transition to the new system.
9. Monitoring and evaluation of the reform's impact.

This is a summary of the proposals in PL 108/2024, which seeks to make Brazil's tax system more efficient, fair, and transparent, benefiting both the government and taxpayers.

What is Split Payment?

"Split Payment" is a new tax payment system proposed by the Tax Reform, particularly through Bill 68/2024. In simple terms, it means "divided payment," and the main idea is that when a sale is made, the tax related to that transaction is automatically separated and directed to the public treasury, instead of being paid by the seller at the end of the month or on a specific date.

How are taxes currently paid?

Currently, a business owner pays the taxes accumulated over the month through a tax collection document, such as the DAS (Simples Nacional Payment Document). This payment usually occurs, for example, on the 20th of the month following the sales. Between the sale and the tax payment, the business owner can use the amount collected to manage cash flow, pay suppliers, salaries, etc.

What changes with Split Payment?

With Split Payment, the amount of taxes (such as CBS and IBS) will be automatically withheld at the time of the transaction. This means that instead of receiving the gross value of the sale, the business owner will receive only the net amount, with the tax already deducted.

Practical Example of a Sale with Split Payment:

Imagine a company selling a product for US$ 1,000, and the tax rate (CBS + IBS) on this sale is 20% (US$ 200). Under the current system, the business owner would receive the full US$ 1,000 and pay the US$ 200 to the government at the end of the month.

With Split Payment, at the moment the customer makes the purchase, the tax amount (US$ 200) is automatically withheld by the platform (such as a credit card machine or a marketplace), which sends this amount directly to the tax authorities. Therefore, the business owner receives US$ 800 instead of US$ 1,000, and the tax is already collected.

How Will Payment to the Supplier and the Tax Authorities Work in Split Payment?

In the Split Payment system, the buyer continues to pay the total amount of the product or service to the supplier, but the payment is automatically divided:

- Part to the supplier: The net amount, after taxes have been deducted.

- Part to the tax authorities: The portion corresponding to the taxes is sent directly to the public treasury.

If, for example, a purchase of US$1,000 is made on a marketplace, the supplier will only be credited with the net US$800, while the US$200 tax will go to the government without passing through the seller's hands.

Cash payment in Split Payment.

If the payment is made in cash, the operation follows the same logic: the customer pays the full amount of the product or service (US$1,000 in the previous example), and the system immediately removes the tax portion (US$200) for the government, passing on the net amount (US$800) to the seller.

Payment in installments in Split Payment.

If the payment is made in installments, Split Payment also withholds taxes as the buyer pays the installments. The important thing here is that the taxes are collected in proportion to each payment made.

Example of payment in installments:

A buyer installs a purchase of US$ 1,000 in 5 installments.

With each payment of US$ 200, the system removes the 20% tax (US$ 40) and forwards it to the tax authorities.

The seller receives the net amount of each installment (US$ 160), and the tax (US$ 40) goes directly to the government.

In this way, the tax authorities collect the taxes as the buyer pays the installments.

Impact of Split Payment on cash flow.

This new model can have a direct impact on the cash flow of entrepreneurs, especially small businesses, which often use the amount of tax that would have been paid at the end of the month to cover other expenses. With Split Payment, the entrepreneur will no longer have access to this amount, as the tax will be withheld immediately.

Conclusion.

Split Payment brings greater control and efficiency to tax collection, preventing tax evasion. However, it also requires entrepreneurs to adjust their financial management, as they will no longer have the flexibility to use the tax amount temporarily. In addition, the system will have to be implemented gradually, which will allow for a less abrupt transition for businesses, especially small ones.

IMPACT OF THE TAX BURDEN.

Taking into account the wide range of products and services covered by Bill 68/2024, the following simulations will use hypothetical IBS and CBS calculation bases, trying to be as comprehensive as possible, regardless of the company's line of business and considering that a supplier may, for example, operate with a tax calculation base of, say, 60%, but the seller may be subject to a calculation base of 100%.

For SIMPLES NACIONAL participants, Bill 68/2024 makes no major changes to tax rates, restricting itself to the percentages of taxes to be credited to federal entities. However, regardless of the rates applied by the SIMPLES NACIONAL, when a SIMPLES company buys from a fully taxed company, it cannot appropriate tax credits.

In other words, the amounts of the credits will be integrated into the prices of the products.

SIMPLES companies, when making a sale to industry or commerce, because of their special reduced tax rates, are not entitled to tax credits under VAT.

Simulations:

1-Fully taxed.

1.1 VAT.

Calculation Base: 100%.

Input Credit: 100%.

In this example, both taxpayers, buyer and seller, are considered to be taxed equally.

1.1.1 Sale from Industry to Industry. VAT.

On input:		**On output: 100% Margin**
Value (+ tax):	126,50	226,50
IBS Calculation Base:	100,00	100,00
CBS Calculation Base:	100,00	100,00
IBS Rate: 17.7%	17,70	35,40
CBS Rate: 8.8%	8,80	17,60
Input Credit/Tax:	26,50	53,00
Tax Burden		**11,69%**

1.1.2 Sale from Industry to Industry. Current system.

On input:		**On output: 100% Margin**
Value of Products + IPI	105,00	210,00
ICMS: BCI 105% Rate 18%	18,90	37,80
IPI: BCI 100% Rate 5%	5,00	10,00
PIS + COFINS: 3.6% *	3,65	7,56
Input Credit/Tax:	23,90	55,36
Tax Burden		**14,98%**

BCI = Tax Calculation Base. * No right to credit.

The value of the IPI, part of the ICMS calculation base, is added to the invoice total but will be passed on to the next operation when the industry sells to the retailer. Therefore, the calculation base for the tax burden is 200.00, not 210.00.

1.2.1 Sale from Industry to Retail. VAT.

On input:		On output: 100% Margin
Value (+ tax):	126,50	226,50
IBS Calculation Base:	100,00	100,00
CBS Calculation Base:	100,00	100,00
IBS Rate: 17.70%	17,70	35,40
CBS Rate: 8.8%	8,80	17,60
Input Credit/Tax:	26,50	53,00
Tax Burden		**11,69%**

The retailer bears the cost of the IPI but does not declare it on the invoice. Instead, it absorbs the tax and, in the next transaction, passes it on to another retailer or the final consumer.

1.2.2 Sale from Industry to Retail. Current system.

On input:		On output: 100% Margin
Value of Products + IPI	105,00	210,00
ICMS: BCI 105% Rate 18%	18,90	37,80
IPI: BCI 100% Rate 5% *	5,00	0
PIS + COFINS: 3,6% *	3,65	7,56
Input Credit/Tax:	18,90	46,20
Tax Burden		**12,6%**

BCI = Tax Calculation Base. * No right to credit.

1.3.1 Sale from Retail to Retail. VAT.

On input:		**On output: 100% Margin**
Value (+ tax):	126,50	226,50
IBS Calculation Base:	100,00	100,00
CBS Calculation Base:	100,00	100,00
IBS Rate: 17.70%	17,70	35,40
CBS Rate: 8.80%	8,80	17,60
Input Credit/Tax:	26,50	53,00
Tax Burden		**11,69%**

In retail-to-retail sales, common transactions between wholesale and retail, the transaction is not taxed by IPI, whose value is theoretically embedded in the prices of both.

1.3.2 Sale from Industry to Retail. Current system.

On input:		**On output: 100% Margin**
Value of Products	105,00	210,00
ICMS: BCI 100% Rate 18%	18,00	37,80
IPI: BCI 100% Rate 5% *	5,00	0
PIS + COFINS: 3.6% *	3,65	7,56
Input Credit/Tax:	18,00	45,36
Tax Burden		**13,02%**

BCI = Tax Calculation Base. * No right to credit.

Sales to the final consumer do not grant tax credit rights.

1.4.1 Sale from Retail to Consumer. VAT.

On input:		On output: 100% Margin
Value (+ tax):	0	126,50
IBS Calculation Base:	0	100
CBS Calculation Base:	0	100
IBS Rate: 17.70%	0	17,70
CBS Rate: 8.8%	0	8,80
Input Credit/Tax:	0	26,50
Tax Burden		**26,50%**

1.4.2 Sale from Retail to Consumer. Current system.

On input:		On output: 100% Margin
Value of Products	100,00	100,00
ICMS: BCI 100% Rate 18%	18,00	18,00
IPI: BCI 100% Rate 5%	0	0
PIS + COFINS: 3.6%	0	0
Input Credit/Tax:	0	0
Tax Burden		**18%**

2. SIMPLES NACIONAL.

2.1 VAT. Calculation Base 100%.
Input Credit 100%.
SIMPLES Rate (4th Bracket): 11.20%.

The purpose of the simulation for SIMPLES NACIONAL is to provide an overview of the impact of PL 68/2024 on the operations of micro and small businesses.

In the first hypothetical example (2.1.1), a broom manufacturer, fully taxed, sells to a company that sells cleaning products and is taxed under the SIMPLES NACIONAL. Then (2.1.2), the same manufacturer makes an identical sale to a large supermarket chain, both taxed under VAT.

In the second example (2.1.2), a company taxed under SIMPLES NACIONAL, also a broom manufacturer, sells to another company under SIMPLES and later sells to a large supermarket chain taxed under VAT. Both manufacturing companies purchase from the same suppliers.

2.1.1 Fully Taxed sells to SIMPLES.

On input:		On output: 100% Margin
Value (+ tax):	126,50	252,00
IBS and CBS Calculation Base:	100,00	0
IBS Rate: 17.70%	17,70	0
CBS Rate: 8.8%	8,80	0
SIMPLES Rate:	11,20	28,22
Input Credit/Tax:	0	0
Tax Burden		**11,20%**

2.1.2 Fully Taxed sells to supermarket..

On input:		On output: 100% Margin
Value (+ tax):	126,50	252,00
IBS and CBS Calculation Base:	100,00	100
IBS Rate: 17.70%	17,70	35,40
CBS Rate: 8.8%	8,80	17,60
Input Credit/Tax:	26,50	26,50
Tax Burden		**10,51%**

The disadvantage for the microenterprise would be even greater if the company were taxed under the 5th Bracket of SIMPLES NACIONAL, which is 14.70%, resulting in a tax burden of 14.70%.

In the last bracket of SIMPLES, which covers a monthly revenue of \$300,000.00 to \$400,000.00, the rate is a modest 29.90%, generating a tax burden of 29.90%.

Passing this percentage (29.90%) on to the final price of the product, we would have, as shown in example 2.1.1, a final price of \$327.00.

In this example (2.1.3.1), we consider that both companies under SIMPLES are in the same tax bracket, where the rate is 14.70%.

2.1.3.1 SIMPLES sells to SIMPLES.

On input:		**On output: 100% Margin**
Value (+ tax):	114,70	229,40
SIMPLES Rate:	14,70	29,40
Input Credit/Tax:	0	0
Tax Burden		**14,70%**

The final price of $229.40 would be competitive enough to face the competition from companies taxed under VAT.

But not if the buying company is taxed at a lower bracket than the selling company. The seller is taxed at 29.90% and the buyer at 14.70% in this example.

2.1.3.2 SIMPLES sells to SIMPLES.

On input:		**On output: 100% Margin**
Value (+ tax):	129,90	259,80
SIMPLES Rate:	29,90	14,70
Input Credit/Tax:	0	38,19
Tax Burden		**15,08%**

However, this is a conservative example. If the tax amount were added to the final sale price, we would have $297.99, with $43.80 in taxes and a tax burden of 14.70%. But the price would be 14% higher than in example 2.1.2.

In example 2.1.4, a company under SIMPLES taxed at the 5th bracket (14.70%) makes a sale to a supermarket taxed under VAT.

The resale price would be $229.40 (cost multiplied by 2) plus $33.51 of VAT. But since the tax amount is added to the sale price, the final price includes the tax itself.

2.1.4 SIMPLES sells to supermarket.

On input:		**On output: 100% Margin**
Value (+ tax):	114,70	277,45
IBS and CBS Calculation Base:	100,00	100,00
IBS Rate: 17.70%	0	49,10
CBS Rate: 8.8%	0	24,41
Input Credit/Tax:	0	73,51
Tax Burden		**26,50%**

Conclusion.

Comparing with item 2.1.2, where a company fully taxed under VAT sells to a supermarket, with a tax burden of 10.51%, and item 1.3.1, retail-to-retail sale under VAT, with a tax burden of 11.69%, the operation under SIMPLES becomes unfeasible by presenting a tax burden of 26.50% for resale to a supermarket taxed under VAT in this example.

However, being optimistic, let's imagine the buyer in this example is willing to use a lower profit margin, thus making the operation viable with the supplier under SIMPLES.

Cost Price of the Merchandise: $114.70.
Profit Margin (60%): $183.36.
VAT (not included): $48.59.
Tax Burden: 26.50%.

Except for the fact that the price would become more competitive, the tax burden would remain the same as in item 2.1.4.

And if we compare it with item 1.2.1, where the operation is taxed under VAT on both ends, we would have a tax burden of 11.69%, which is much lower, with a 100% profit margin.

TAXATION BY TAX SUBSTITUTION.

Because the Tax Reform introduces significant changes to the Brazilian fiscal landscape, it preserves certain mechanisms that remain crucial for maintaining revenue balance, such as tax substitution, mentioned in Article 380 of PL 68/2024. This article ensures the continuity of PIS and COFINS credit appropriations under CBS (Contribution on Goods and Services), even after the elimination of these taxes.

Tax substitution is an efficient mechanism for simplifying tax collection, and despite the innovations brought by the reform, its retention is justified in sectors with a large number of taxpayers and products that are difficult to control fiscally. With CBS, the appropriation of presumed credits will incorporate previous legal provisions, ensuring that companies already using this mechanism are not adversely affected.

Additionally, Article 380 reinforces legal certainty for companies, guaranteeing that credits arising from depreciation, amortization, or monthly quotas will be preserved. This demonstrates an effort toward continuity and adaptation of the new legislation, avoiding abrupt disruption of acquired rights and enabling a smooth transition to the new tax system.

By mentioning this article in this book, we highlight the relevance of tax substitution and its importance for the tax planning of companies, software developers, and public administrators, providing a clear overview of the changes that will occur and the mechanisms that will be maintained.

Tax Substitution (ST) is a mechanism used by the government to facilitate the collection of ICMS. It consists of the anticipation of tax payment at an earlier point in the goods or services distribution chain. Thus, the tax is collected at an initial stage (usually from the manufacturer or importer), even though the goods will go through several stages before reaching the final consumer.

This mechanism is widely used in sectors with a large number of resellers, such as alcoholic beverages, fuels, and cigarettes, for example.

Types of Tax Substitution:

1. Forward Tax Substitution (STF): the tax is collected at the initial stage and applies to all subsequent stages of the production chain until the sale to the final consumer.

2. Backward Tax Substitution (STT): the tax is collected at a stage after the taxable event has occurred, generally applied under a deferral regime.

3. Concurrent Tax Substitution (STC): occurs when the tax is collected simultaneously with the occurrence of the taxable event of the transaction.

Calculation of Forward Tax Substitution (STF).

The calculation of ICMS-ST follows the following formula:

ICMS-ST = (Presumed Final Sale Price × ICMS Rate)-Own ICMS

Where:

Presumed Final Sale Price: this is the estimated sale price to the final consumer, including the Added Value Margin (MVA).

ICMS Rate: this is the percentage of the tax that will be applied to the transaction.

Own ICMS: this is the ICMS that the taxpayer has already collected on their own sale.

Step-by-step calculation:

1. Presumed Final Sale Price:

$$pFinalSale = pSaleManufacturer \times (1 + MVA)$$

The final sale price is obtained by applying the MVA to the manufacturer's sale price. The MVA is a presumed margin that indicates how much the value of the merchandise should increase until it reaches the final consumer.

2. Calculation of ICMS on the Presumed Final Price:

$$ICMS_{Final} = PFinalSale \times ICMS\ Rate$$

The final ICMS is calculated on the presumed sale price.

3. Subtraction of Own ICMS:

$$ICMSST = ICMS_{Final} - Own\ ICMS$$

Finally, the value of ICMS-ST is obtained by subtracting the ICMS already collected by the manufacturer on their transaction.

Example Calculation:

Suppose a beverage manufacturer sells a batch of soft drinks to a distributor for $1,000.00, and the MVA for this product is 30%. The ICMS rate is 18%.

1. Presumed Final Price:

$$PFinalSale = 1,000.00 \times (1 + 0.30) = 1,300.00$$

The presumed final price for the consumer is $1,300.00.

2. ICMS on the Presumed Final Price:

$$ICMS_{Final} = 1,300.00 \times 18\% = 234.00$$

The ICMS on the presumed final price is $234.00.

3. Own ICMS:

The ICMS that the manufacturer has already collected on their own sale is:

$$ICMSOwn = 1,000.00 \times 18\% = 180.00$$

The own ICMS is $180.00.

4. ICMS-ST Amount:

$$ICMSST = 234.00 - 180.00 = 54.00$$

The ICMS-ST amount to be collected by the manufacturer is $54.00.

Examples of NF-e XML File.

1. Internal Operation (within the same state).

Tag XML	Commentary
<imposto>	Start of the block of tax information.
<ICMS>	Start of the ICMS section.
<ICMSST>	Indicates that ICMS is taxed through tax substitution.
<orig>	Code for the origin of the goods (1 for National, 2 for Foreign).
<CST>	Tax Situation Code (70 for internal tax substitution).
<vBC>	ICMS calculation base.
<pICMS>	Applicable ICMS rate.
<vICMS>	Calculated ICMS value.
<vBCST>	ICMS tax substitution calculation base.
<pICMSST>	ICMS tax substitution rate.
<vICMSST>	ICMS tax substitution value.
</ICMSST>	End of ICMS tax substitution section.
</ICMS>	End of ICMS section.
</imposto>	End of the block of tax information.

XML Example:

```
<imposto>
<ICMS>
<ICMSST>
<orig>1</orig>
<CST>70</CST>
<vBC>1000.00</vBC>
<pICMS>18.00</pICMS>
<vICMS>180.00</vICMS>
<vBCST>1000.00</vBCST>
<pICMSST>18.00</pICMSST>
<vICMSST>180.00</vICMSST>
</ICMSST>
</ICMS>
</imposto>
```

2. Interstate Operation (to another state of the federation).

Tag XML	Commentary
<imposto>	Tax information block start
<ICMS>	ICMS section start
<ICMSST>	Indicates that ICMS is subject to substitute taxation.
<orig>	Origin code of the merchandise (1 for Domestic, 2 for Foreign).
<CST>	Tax Situation Code (70 for interstate substitute taxation)
<vBC>	ICMS calculation base
<pICMS>	Applicable ICMS rate

<vICMS>	Calculated ICMS value
<vBCST>	ICMS tax substitution calculation base.
<pICMSST>	ICMS tax substitution rate.
<vICMSST>	ICMS tax substitution value.
<vBCUFDest>	ICMS tax substitution calculation base for the destination state.
<pICMSUFDest>	ICMS tax substitution rate for the destination state.
<vICMSUFDest>	ICMS tax substitution value for the destination state.
</ICMSST>	End of ICMS tax substitution section.
</ICMS>	End of ICMS section.
</imposto>	Tax information block end

XML Example (interstate operation):

```
<imposto>

<ICMS>

<ICMSST>

<orig>1</orig>

<CST>70</CST>

<vBC>1000.00</vBC>

<pICMS>18.00</pICMS>

<vICMS>180.00</vICMS>

<vBCST>1000.00</vBCST>
```

```xml
 <pICMSST>18.00</pICMSST>

<vICMSST>180.00</vICMSST>

<vBCUFDest>1000.00</vBCUFDest>

<pICMSUFDest>2.00</pICMSUFDest>

<vICMSUFDest>20.00</vICMSUFDest>

</ICMSST>

</ICMS>

</imposto>
```

IMPACT ON E-INVOICE ISSUANCE.

The impact of the Tax Reform on the issuance of Electronic Invoices – NF-e will be such that, to facilitate understanding, the topic will be divided into three sections: the current NF-e, the NF-e during the transition period, which is the most complex, and the VAT NF-e, hypothetically called version 5.0.

1. Current NF-e.

The following fragment, from a duly authorized version 4.0 NF-e, contains the complete <impostos> (tax) tag from a sales transaction by an industry in the state of São Paulo to a commercial company in the state of Rio Grande do Sul.

```
<imposto>
<ICMS>
<ICMS00>
<orig>0</orig>
<CST>00</CST>
<modBC>3</modBC>
<vBC>6493.50</vBC>
<pICMS>12.00</pICMS>
<vICMS>779.22</vICMS>
</ICMS00>
</ICMS>
<IPI>
```

```xml
<cEnq>999</cEnq>
<IPITrib>
<CST>50</CST>
<vBC>6493.50</vBC>
<pIPI>3.25</pIPI>
<vIPI>211.04</vIPI>
</IPITrib>
</IPI>
<PIS>
<PISAliq>
<CST>01</CST>
<vBC>5714.28</vBC>
<pPIS>1.65</pPIS>
<vPIS>94.29</vPIS>
</PISAliq>
</PIS>
<COFINS>
<COFINSAliq>
<CST>01</CST>
<vBC>5714.28</vBC>
<pCOFINS>7.60</pCOFINS>
<vCOFINS>434.29</vCOFINS>
</COFINSAliq>
</COFINS>
</imposto>
```

There is a deliberate subtlety in the "tags" pPIS and pCOFINS, highlighted in bold.

The issuing company is taxed under the Real Profit system. In terms of PIS and COFINS, this means it collects taxes at a higher rate (1.65% for PIS and 7.60% for COFINS) than a company taxed under the Presumed Profit system (0.65% for PIS and 3.00% for COFINS), but with credit recovery, like any value-added tax.

This fiscal strategy is appropriate for companies operating with small profit margins.

2. Transition Period.

During this presumed 5-year transition period, ICMS (including tax substitution), PIS, COFINS, and IPI will coexist alongside the IBS and CBS of VAT.

The percentages related to VAT will be gradually introduced, starting at 20%, then 40%, and so on until the old taxes are phased out and only VAT remains in use.

In this hypothetical example of issuing an NF-e based on PL 68/2024, during the transition period starting in 2027, the calculation bases of the current taxes (ICMS, IPI, PIS, COFINS) are reduced.

In 2027, part of the tax bases (20% in this example) will migrate to the new IBS/CBS system. Thus, the bases of the old taxes will be reduced while an equivalent percentage is applied to the new taxes.

- *IBS and CBS: The new taxes receive the portion subtracted from the bases of the old taxes. In the example, 20% of the 2027 tax base (i.e., 1298.70) is taxed by IBS and CBS, with respective rates of 17.70% and 8.80%.*

Tag XML	Commentary
<imposto>	
<ICMS>	
<ICMS00>	
<orig>0</orig>	
<CST>00</CST>	
<modBC>3</modBC>	
<vBC>5194.80</vBC>	Reduction of the calculation base by 20% (IBS/CBS included in 2027)
<pICMS>12.00</pICMS>	
<vICMS>623.38</vICMS>	ICMS value with reduced base
</ICMS00>	
</ICMS>	
<IPI>	
<cEnq>999</cEnq>	
<IPITrib>	
<CST>50</CST>	
<vBC>5194.80</vBC>	Reduction of the calculation base by 20%
<pIPI>3.25</pIPI>	
<vIPI>168.83</vIPI>	IPI value with reduced bas
</IPITrib>	
</IPI>	
<PIS>	
<PISAliq>	

`<CST>01</CST>`	
`<vBC>4571.42</vBC>`	Reduction of 20% of the PIS calculation base
`<pPIS>1.65</pPIS>`	

Impact on e-Invoice Issuance

`<vPIS>75.43</vPIS>`	PIS value with reduced base
`</PISAliq>`	
`</PIS>`	
`<COFINS>`	
`<COFINSAliq>`	
`<CST>01</CST>`	
`<vBC>4571.42</vBC>`	Reduction of 20% of the COFINS calculation base
`<pCOFINS>7.60</pCOFINS>`	
`<vCOFINS>347.43</vCOFINS>`	COFINS value with reduced base
`</COFINSAliq>`	
`</COFINS>`	
`<IVA>`	
`<IBS>`	
`<vBCIBS>1298.70</vBCIBS>`	Base de cálculo equivalente a 20% da base original Calculation base equivalent to 20% of the original base
`<pIBS>10.00</pIBS>`	
`<vIBS>129.87</vIBS>`	IBS value calculated
`</IBS>`	
`<CBS>`	
`<vBCCBS>1298.70</vBCCBS>`	Calculation base equivalent to 20% of the original base
`<pCBS>4.00</pCBS>`	
`<vCBS>51.95</vCBS>`	Valor do CBS calculado CBS value calculated
`</CBS>`	
`<IVAcredit>CNPJ ou CPF</IVAcredit>`	Identification of the VAT Creditor (1)*
`<modIVA>1</modIVA>`	VAT included in the total of the NF-e = 1 inside, = 0 outside (2)
`<pIVA>14.00</pIVA>`	Total VAT rate (10% IBS + 4% CBS) → (3)
`<vBCIVA>1298.70</vBCIVA>`	Calculation base for VAT (20% of the original

```
<vPIS>75.43</vPIS>            PIS value with reduced base
                              base) → (4)

</IVA>
<RespTrib>ID</RespTrib>       ID of the Tax Responsible Party
</imposto>
```

*CPF (Cadastro de Pessoas Físicas): The CPF is a tax identification number for individuals in Brazil. It's similar to a Social Security Number (SSN) in the United States. Every Brazilian citizen and resident is required to have a CPF for tax purposes, as well as for a variety of other financial and legal transactions.

*CNPJ (Cadastro Nacional Sam da Pessoa Jurídica): The CNPJ is the national tax identification number for businesses in Brazil. It's similar to the Employer Identification Number (EIN) used by businesses in the United States. All legal entities, including companies, organizations, and non-profits, must have a CNPJ to operate legally in Brazil.

The following hypothetical "tags" indicate the method of calculation and the recipient of the VAT credit when purchases are made.

1. **<IVAcredit>**: there are companies with branches across the country. Many of them have centralized purchasing. Depending on the tax regime to which the company is subject, it may choose which of its branches it wants the VAT credits to be directed to. Simply provide the CNPJ or CPF of the credited company.

2. **<modIVA>**: this is a "tag" to indicate how the VAT will be calculated. 1 = Inside. This means that the tax amount is included in the total value of the NF-e. And 0 = Outside. This means that the tax amount will be added to the total value of the goods or services.

3. **<*pIVA*>**: The total VAT rate; the sum of the CBS and IBS rates.

4. **<*vBCIVA*>**: Value of the VAT calculation base. In this example of a transition operation, 20%.

5. **<*vIVA*>**: Value of the VAT.

The graphical representation (figure 1) of this hypothetical NF-e example follows:

imposto
ICMS
ICMS00
orig 0
CST 00
modBC 3
vBC 5194.80
pICMS 12.00
vICMS 623.38
IPI
cEnq 999
IPITrib
CST 50
vBC 5194.80
pIPI 3.25
vIPI 168.83
PIS
PISAliq
CST 01
vBC 4571.42
pPIS 1.65
vPIS 75.43
COFINS
COFINSAliq
CST 01
vBC 4571.42
pCOFINS 7.60
vCOFINS 347.43
IVA
IBS
vBCIBS 1298.70
pIBS 10.00
vIBS 129.87
CBS
vBCCBS 1298.70
pCBS 4.00
vCBS 51.95
IVAcredit 00000000000000
modIVA 1
vBCIVA 1298.70
pIVA 14.00
vIVA 181.82

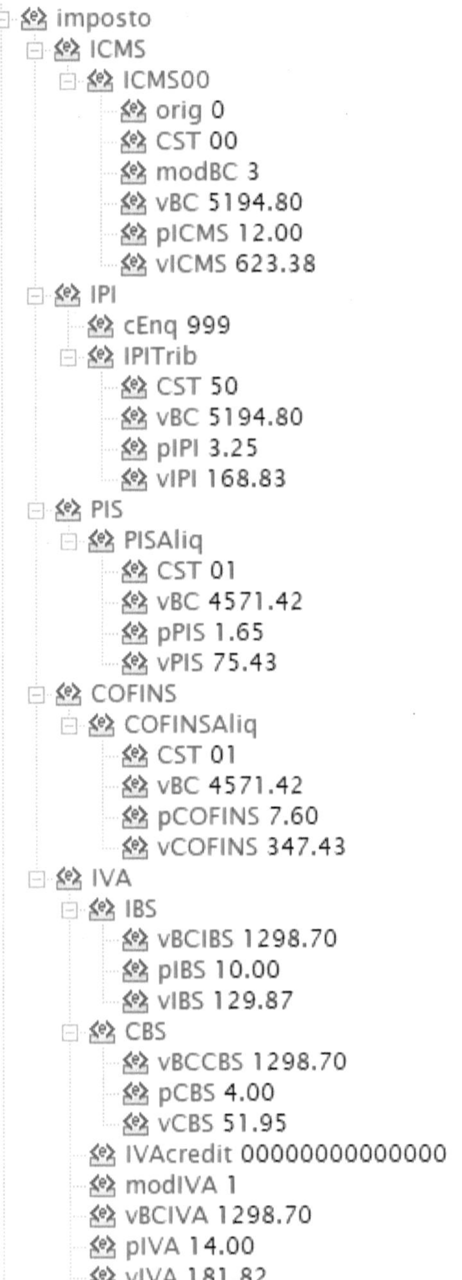

Figure 1.

3. NF-e VAT.

A hypothetical example of issuing an NF-e based on PL 68/2024, fully implemented:

Tags XML	Commentary
<imposto>	
<IVA>	
<IVAcredit>CNPJ/CPF </IVAcredit>	Identification of the VAT Creditor*
<modIVA>1</modIVA>	VAT included in the total of the NF-e = 1 inside, 0 outside (2)
<vBCIVA>1000.00</vBCIVA>	Total calculation base for VAT
<pIVA>26.50</pIVA>	Total VAT rate, composed of IBS and CBS
<vIVA>265.00</vIVA>	Total VAT value calculated
<IBS>	
<vBCIBS>1000.00</vBCIBS>	IBS calculation base (100%)
<pIBS>17.70</pIBS>	IBS rate
<vIBS>177.00</vIBS>	IBS value calculated
</IBS>	
<CBS>	
<vBCCBS>1000.00</vBCCBS>	CBS calculation base (100%)
<pCBS>8.80</pCBS>	CBS rate
<vCBS>88.00</vCBS>	CBS value calculated
</CBS>	
</IVA>	
<IS>	Selective Tax
<vBCIS>0.00</vBCIS>	Calculation base for IS (Selective Tax)
<pIS>0.00</pIS>	IS rate (0%)
<vIS>0.00</vIS>	IS value calculated
</IS>	
<RespTrib>ID</RespTrib>	ID of the Tax Responsible Party
<TotImp>265.00</TotImp>	Total tax of the item
</imposto>	

- ***VAT (IVA)***: *Replaces ICMS, IPI, PIS, and COFINS, and includes the corresponding values for IBS and CBS.*
- ***IBS***: *Total calculation base, with a rate of 17.70%.*
- ***CBS***: *Total calculation base, with a rate of 8.80%.*
- ***IS (Selective Tax)***: *A selective tax, with a 0% rate in this case, which may vary in specific operations.*

- *Graphical representation of the NF-e XML file (Figure 2).*

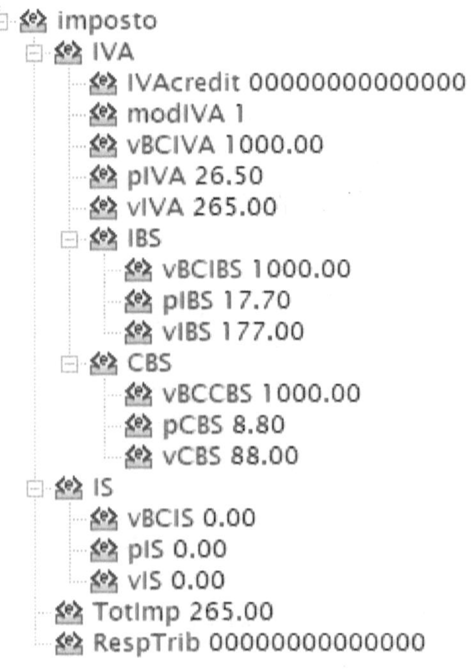

Figure 2.

SERVICE PROVIDERS.

In order to provide an overview of the new taxation on services, we will analyze the relevant aspects of Chapter II of PL 68/2024.

As we will see below in Chapter II, the IBS and CBS rates will be reduced by 30% for individuals and legal entities. This means that the tax burden on the services listed below will be 18.55%, lower compared to the taxation under the SIMPLES NACIONAL, depending on the tax bracket.

CHAPTER II.
ON THE THIRTY PERCENT REDUCTION OF IBS AND CBS RATES.

Art. 122. The IBS and CBS rates levied on the provision of services by the following intellectual professions of a scientific, literary, or artistic nature, subject to professional council supervision, are hereby reduced by 30% (thirty percent):

I-administrators;
II-lawyers;
III-architects and urban planners;
IV-social workers;
V-librarians;
VI-biologists;
VII-accountants;

VIII-economists;

IX-home economists;

X-physical education professionals;

XI-engineers and agronomists;

XII-statisticians;

XIII-veterinarians and animal scientists;

XIV-museologists;

XV-chemists;

XVI-public relations professionals;

XVII-industrial technicians; and

XVIII-agricultural technicians.

§ 1º The rate reduction provided for in the caput of this article applies to:

I-the provision of services by individuals, provided that the services rendered are linked to the professionals' qualifications; and

II-the provision of services by legal entities that meet all the following requirements:

a) the partners must hold professional qualifications directly related to the company's objectives and be subject to professional council supervision;

b) there are no legal entities as partners;

c) the entity is not a partner of another legal entity;

d) the company does not engage in activities unrelated to the professional qualifications of the partners; and

e) the services related to the core business are provided directly by the partners, with the support of assistants or collaborators.

§ 2º For the purposes of the provisions of item II of § 1º of this article, the following do not prevent the rate reduction referred to in this article:

I-the legal nature of the company;

II-the combination of different professions provided for in items I to XVIII of the caput of this article, as long as each partner operates within their professional qualification; and

III-the method of profit distribution.

ANNEX II.

Annex II deals with the 60% reduction of IBS and CBS rates for services related to education and health, as shown in the table below:

ITEM	DESCRIPTION OF SERVICE	NBS
1	Early Childhood Education, including daycare and preschool	1.2201.1
2	Elementary Education	1.2201.20.00
3	Secondary Education	1.2201.30.00
4	Technical Secondary Education	1.2202.00.00
5	Education for youth and adults who did not have access to or continue their studies in elementary and secondary education at the appropriate age	1.2203
6	Higher Education, including undergraduate, postgraduate, extension programs, and sequential courses	1.2204
7	Education of sign language and tactile writing systems	1.2205.13.00
8	Education of native languages of indigenous peoples	1.2205.13.00
9	Special education for people with disabilities, global developmental disorders, and high abilities or giftedness, either in isolation or in combination with any of the educational stages covered in this Annex	

* Brazilian Service Nomenclature

ANNEX III.

Annex III deals with the 60% reduction of IBS and CBS rates for services related to health, as shown in the table below:

ITEM	DESCRIPTION OF SERVICE	NBS(*)
1	Surgical services	1.2301.11.00
2	Gynecological and obstetric services	1.2301.12.00
3	Psychiatric services	1.2301.13.00
4	Services provided in Intensive Care Units	1.2301.14.00
5	Emergency care services	1.2301.15.00
6	Hospital services not classified in previous subheadings	1.2301.19.00
7	Medical clinic services	1.2301.21.00
8	Specialized medical services	1.2301.22.00
9	Dental services	1.2301.23.00
10	Nursing services	1.2301.91.00
11	Physiotherapy services	1.2301.92.00
12	Laboratory services	1.2301.93.00
13	Imaging diagnostic services	1.2301.94.00
14	Human biological material bank services	1.2301.95.00
15	Ambulance services	1.2301.96.00
16	Childbirth and postpartum care services	1.2301.97.00
17	Psychology services	1.2301.98.00
18	Public health surveillance services	1.2301.99.00
19	Epidemiology services	1.2301.99.00
20	Vaccination services	1.2301.99.00

ITEM	DESCRIPTION OF SERVICE	NBS(*)
21	Speech therapy services	1.2301.99.00
22	Nutrition services	1.2301.99.00
23	Optometry services	1.2301.99.00
24	Surgical instrumentation services	1.2301.99.00
25	Bio-medicine services	1.2301.99.00
26	Pharmaceutical services	1.2301.99.00
27	Care and assistance services for the elderly and people with disabilities in care facilities	1.2302

* Brazilian Service Nomenclature

IMPACT OF PL 68/2024.

Given that PL 68/2024 contains more than 400 pages, we will present an educational summary obtained from the gov.br website and, at the end of this section, an index of the chapters of the law.

Here are the links to the documents of PL 68/2024:

FINAL DRAFT FROM THE CHAMBER OF DEPUTIES
link:
https://legis.senado.leg.br/sdleg-getter/documento?
dm=9725946&ts=1725410367618&disposition=inline

PROCESSING IN THE FEDERAL SENATE
link:
https://www25.senado.leg.br/web/atividade/materias/-/
materia/164914#tramitacao_10875162

IBS AND CBS ON OPERATIONS.

1) Taxable Event.

The IBS and CBS apply to all onerous transactions involving goods and services. The operations on which IBS and CBS are levied include the provision of goods and services and may arise from any legal act or business transaction. For legal certainty regarding the scope of IBS and CBS, PL 68/2024 includes the following illustrative list of legal acts and business transactions that involve the provision of goods or services and that will therefore be subject to IBS and CBS:

Impact of PL 68/2024.

- alienation, including purchase and sale, exchange or barter, and dation in payment;
- leasing;
- licensing, granting, cession;
- loan;
- onerous donation;
- onerous establishment of real rights;
- leasing, including finance leasing; and
- provision of services.

As provided for by Constitutional Amendment (EC) 32/2023, PL 68/2024 defines a transaction with a service as any operation that is not classified as a transaction with a good. Therefore, any supply that does not involve a material or immaterial good, including a right, will be considered a transaction with a service.

The IBS and CBS also apply to certain non-onerous operations or those carried out at a value below market value, such as the provision of goods and services for personal use and consumption by the taxpayer, if an individual, or by employees and administrators of the taxpayer, when the taxpayer is not an individual. Goods and services provided for personal use and consumption are considered to include the availability of real estate, vehicles, and communication equipment, communication services, health care plans, education, food and beverages, and insurance. Goods and services used exclusively in the taxpayer's economic activity are not considered for personal use and consumption, and the criteria for this determination will be established by regulation.

In addition to constitutional immunities, no tax is levied on services rendered by individuals in the capacity of employees, administrators, or members of advisory boards and committees as provided by law. The transfer of goods between the taxpayer's establishments is also not subject to taxation. IBS and CBS do not apply to the transfer of corporate shares, nor to the transfer of assets resulting from mergers, spin-offs, and incorporations, or from capital contributions and returns. Financial income, transactions with securities, and the receipt of dividends and other corporate participation results are not subject to IBS and CBS, except as provided for under the specific financial services regime. However, IBS and CBS may apply to arrangements involving a combination of legal acts and transactions if they essentially constitute an onerous transaction with goods or services (anti-abuse rule).

2) Occurrence of the Taxable Event.

The moment when the tax applies to a transaction, that is, the taxable event for IBS and CBS, is generally determined by whichever occurs first: the supply or the payment.

For services such as water, sanitation, gas, communication, and electricity, as well as for those that are continuous or fragmented, the taxable event occurs when the payment becomes due, especially when it is not possible to clearly identify the exact moment of delivery or completion of the service.

The supply of a transportation service that begins in the country is considered to occur at the moment the transportation begins, while for other services, the supply is considered completed at the moment of finalization.

3) Location of the Operation.

Defining the location where the taxable event occurs is crucial to determine the applicable tax rate and how the collected revenue will be distributed. The location varies according to the type of good or service involved in the transaction, as shown in the table below:

Type/Object of Supply	Location of the Operation
Movable tangible good availability of the good to the recipient	

Immovable good, immaterial movable good (including rights), related to immovable property and service provided on immovable property	Location where the property is situated
Service physically provided to an individual or enjoyed in person by an individual	Location of the provision of the service
Service of planning, organization, and management of fairs, exhibitions, congresses, shows, displays, and similar events	Location of the event to which the service refers
Service provided on movable tangible goods	Location of the provision of the service
Passenger transportation service	Location where the transportation begins
Cargo transportation service	Location of delivery or availability of the good to the recipient
Highway exploitation service with the collection of fees or tolls	The territory of each Municipality and State, or the Federal District, proportionate to the corresponding length of the highway explored
Communication service where there is transmission through-physical means received	Location where the service is
Other services and other immaterial movable goods, including rights domicile	Location of the recipient's primary

Recipient's Primary Domicile.

PL 68/2024 defines the recipient's primary domicile as the location registered in official records. For individuals, it is considered the place of permanent residence or, in the absence of such, the location where their economic relations are most significant. For legal entities, the primary domicile is the location of each establishment that receives immaterial goods or services.

In cases of centralized acquisitions by taxpayers with multiple establishments, the primary domicile will be that of the main establishment, meaning the one where the economic relations are most significant. For unregistered recipients, the law provides specific criteria to determine the primary domicile.

4) Calculation Base.

The calculation base for IBS and CBS is the value of the transaction, which includes the full amount charged by the supplier for any reason, including: increases due to adjustments in the transaction value, interest, penalties, surcharges and fees, conditional discounts, the value of transportation charged as part of the transaction value, taxes and public charges, including tariffs, except those expressly excluded, and all other amounts charged or received as part of the transaction value, including insurance and fees.

PL 68/2024 stipulates the exclusion from the calculation base of the amount corresponding to IBS and CBS themselves, IPI, unconditional discounts, and reimbursements or refunds received for amounts paid related to operations carried out on behalf of or in the name of third parties, provided that the tax documentation for these operations is issued in the name of the third party. During the transition period, from January 1, 2026, to December 31, 2032, the amounts of ISS, ICMS, PIS, and COFINS are also excluded from the calculation base for IBS and CBS.

In some cases, the calculation base will correspond to the market value of goods or services, understood as the value practiced in comparable transactions between unrelated parties. The market value will be applied when the transaction has no value, the value is undetermined or not represented in money, or when the transaction is between related parties.

5) Rates.

The CBS and IBS rates will be set by specific laws of the respective entities, and each entity will individually set its own rate, which must be the same for all transactions involving goods and services occurring in that location, unless subject to differentiated or specific regimes. When setting its own rate, each entity of the federation may:

- link it to the reference rate of the respective federal entity, by means of an increase or decrease to the reference rate in percentage points, or

- define it without linking it to the reference rate of the respective federal entity.

If the entity does not establish its rate through specific law, the reference rate of the respective federal entity will apply. The IBS rate applied to each transaction will correspond to the sum of the rates of the State and Municipality, or the Federal District, of the destination of the transaction, determined according to the rules of the location of the operation.

6) Taxpayer Subjects.

The taxpayer for IBS and CBS is the supplier who engages in transactions:

- in the course of economic activity;
- habitually or in volumes that characterize economic activity; or
- professionally, even if the profession is not regulated.

Additionally, anyone expressly mentioned in other provisions of PL 68/2024, even if not meeting these requirements, is considered a taxpayer. PL 68/2024 also stipulates that the supplier, resident or domiciled abroad, is a taxpayer of IBS and CBS and is required to register under the regular regime for operations occurring in Brazil.

The taxpayer is required to register in the IBS and CBS registries. Furthermore, the taxpayer is subject to the regular IBS and CBS regime, unless they opt for the Special Unified Tax Collection Regime for Micro and Small Businesses – Simples Nacional, or the Individual Microentrepreneur Regime – MEI, as established by Complementary Law No. 123 of December 14, 2006. The regular IBS and CBS regime includes not only transactions subject to the general rules of IBS and CBS but also those applicable to differentiated and specific regimes. Taxpayers opting for Simples Nacional or MEI are subject to the rules of these regimes.

PL 68/2024 stipulates that residential condominiums, consortia, and partnership companies are not taxpayers of IBS and CBS. These non-legal entities may, optionally, register as taxpayers.

Responsible Parties.

Digital platforms, even those domiciled abroad, are responsible for collecting IBS and CBS related to operations carried out through their intermediary. The responsibility will substitute the supplier, if the supplier is a resident or domiciled abroad. In this case, the foreign supplier is exempt from registration in the IBS and CBS registries if they conduct operations exclusively through a digital platform. In cases where the supplier is a resident or domiciled in Brazil, the platform will be jointly responsible with the supplier if the latter is not registered for IBS and CBS or does not record the operation in an electronic tax document.

PL 68/2024 defines a digital platform as one that acts as an intermediary between suppliers and purchasers in non-face-to-face or electronic operations and controls one or more of the following essential elements of the transaction, such as billing, payment, defining terms and conditions, or delivery. A platform is not considered digital if it only provides internet access, payment processing, advertising, or supplier search or comparison, as long as it does not charge for the service based on sales made. PL 68/2024 also provides a list of other instances of tax liability, in addition to those provided for in the National Tax Code and civil legislation, including the Civil Code, which will cover the payment of IBS and CBS, including monetary correction and updates, late fees, punitive fines, and other charges.

7) Payment of IBS and CBS.

PL 68/2024 provides the following payment methods for IBS and CBS levied on transactions involving goods or services:

- offset with IBS and CBS credits appropriated by the taxpayer;
- payment by the taxpayer, including through remittance;

• remittance upon financial settlement of the transaction (split payment);
• remittance by the purchaser; and
• remittance by the responsible party.

8) Non-cumulativity.

A taxpayer registered under the regular regime may appropriate credits when payment is made, by any of the methods described above, of the IBS and CBS amounts levied on transactions in which the taxpayer is the purchaser of goods or services. Credit appropriation by the taxpayer is prohibited in the acquisition of goods and services considered for personal use or consumption and in other cases expressly provided for in PLP 68/2024, such as cases of exemption and immunity and specific regimes.

For the purposes of credit prohibition, goods and services for personal use and consumption include the acquisition of jewelry, precious stones and metals; works of art and antiques of historical or archaeological value; alcoholic beverages; tobacco products; weapons and ammunition; and recreational, sporting, and aesthetic goods and services, except when necessary for the taxpayer's operations.

Operations that are exempt, immune, or subject to a zero rate will not allow credit appropriation for use in subsequent operations ("forward credit"), as there was no payment of IBS and CBS in the operation and, therefore, there is no value to be credited. In cases of deferral or suspension, crediting will only be allowed at the time of actual tax payment. Regarding credit on acquisitions ("backward credit"), the exemption or immunity of goods and services will result in the cancellation of the credit related to the supplier's previous operations. In the case of exports, however, acquisition credits are constitutionally guaranteed. If a supplier conducts exempt or immune operations as well as operations taxable by IBS and CBS, the cancellation of "backward" credits will be proportional to the value of the exempt and immune operations in relation to the total value of the supplier's operations. For operations subject to a zero rate, the credit related to the supplier's acquisitions will be maintained.

PL 68/2024 establishes a five-year period for the utilization of credits and prohibits the transfer of credits, except in cases of universal succession, merger, spin-off, or incorporation, preserving the original date for calculating the credit utilization period.

9) Simples Nacional.

The taxpayer opting for the Simples Nacional regime may choose to calculate and pay IBS and CBS under the regular regime. If the taxpayer does not choose the regular regime and IBS and CBS are collected through Simples Nacional:

- credit appropriation of IBS and CBS by the Simples Nacional taxpayer will not be allowed; and

- a taxpayer under the regular IBS and CBS regime will be allowed to appropriate credits corresponding to the amounts of these taxes paid on the acquisition of goods and services from a Simples Nacional taxpayer, in an amount equivalent to what is due under that regime.

Summary – Differentiated Regimes.

Reduced IBS and CBS rates.

30% Reduction.

Regulated professions overseen by councils:

I-administrators; II-lawyers; III-architects and urban planners; IV-social workers; V-librarians; VI-biologists; VII-accountants; VIII-economists; IX-home economists; X-physical education professionals; XI-engineers and agronomists; XII-statisticians; XIII-veterinarians and animal scientists; XIV-museologists; XV-chemists; XVI-public relations professionals; XVII-industrial technicians; and XVIII-agricultural technicians.

Regulated professions overseen by professional councils related to the healthcare sector are entitled to a 60% rate reduction, granted to healthcare services.
Redução em 60%.

- Medical devices (92)
- Accessibility devices (26)
- Medications (850)
- Enteral and parenteral compositions (71)
- Basic menstrual health care products (all)
Fast track: for the above types of goods, there is the possibility of annual updates to include medical devices and medications, provided the defined requirements are met
- Education services
- Health services (27)
- Food intended for human consumption (14)

• Hygiene and cleaning products mainly consumed by low-income families (6)
• Agricultural, aquaculture, fishing, forestry, and in natura plant extractive products
• Agricultural and aquaculture inputs (25)
• National artistic, cultural, event, journalistic, and audiovisual productions (25)
• Sports activities
• Institutional communication (public administration)
• Goods and services related to national sovereignty and security, information security, and cybersecurity (33 – public administration)
• Operations related to urban rehabilitation projects in historical zones and critical areas of urban recovery and reconversion

The numbers in parentheses refer to the quantity of items benefiting from the reduction.

Reduction to ZERO.

• Medical devices (33)
• Accessibility devices (7)
• Medications (383)
• Enteral and parenteral compositions
• Basic menstrual health care products

Public purchases:
For the acquisition of the above types of goods, the items listed in the 60% reduction annexes will also be reduced to zero.

Impact of PL 68/2024

Fast track: For the above types of goods, there is the possibility of annual or emergency updates for the inclusion of medical devices and medications, provided the defined requirements are met.
• Services provided by non-profit Scientific, Technological, and Innovation Institutions (ICT)
• Automobiles purchased by people with disabilities and individuals with autism spectrum disorder or by taxi drivers
The numbers in parentheses refer to the quantity of items benefiting from the reduction.

Exemption.

• Urban, semi-urban, or metropolitan collective road passenger transport.

Presumed credits.

• Rural producer and integrated rural producer with annual revenue below US$ 3.6 million
• Independent freight carrier, individual, non-taxpayer
• Waste and other materials destined for recycling, reuse, or reverse logistics acquired from an individual, cooperative, or other form of organization
• Movable goods for resale.

Impact of PL 68/2024

Specific Fuel Regime.
General Characteristics of the Regime.

Characteristic	Description
Nature of the Tax	Monophase (single incidence in the supply chain)
Covered Fuels	All existing and future fuels, as defined by ANP. Lubricants not included.
Calculation Base	Quantity of fuel in the transaction
Rates	Ad rem, uniform across the country, specific per product, with annual adjustment
Criteria for setting the rates	Maintenance of the current tax burden, gradual until 2033
Disclosure of the rates	IBS: Managing Committee; CBS: Head of the Union Executive Branch
Biofuels and Hydrogen	Specific rates to ensure competitiveness
Taxpayers	Producers, refineries, formulators, importers, etc.
Subsidiary Liability	Chain participants who contribute to non-payment

Specific Rules for Biodiesel and Anhydrous Ethanol.

Situation	Tax Responsible Party	Notes
Biodiesel and Anhydrous Ethanol Fuel	Refinery, CPQ, formulator, importer	Responsibility proportional to the percentage of biofuel in the mixture

Situation	Tax Responsible Party	Notes
Biodiesel and Anhydrous Ethanol for blending- Purchaser	Purchaser promoting a different use	Payment of IBS and CBS according to the blending percentage
IBS and CBS Credit	Companies consuming fuel (except for distribution, commercialization, etc.)	Credit guaranteed for exports

Specific Regime for Real Estate Transactions Rate reduced to 20%.

Taxable Event	Occurrence	Calculation Base	Taxpayer
Real Estate Disposal, including from real estate incorporation and land subdivision	At the moment of disposal or upon execution, including any subsequent adjustments, of the disposal contract, whether by means of a promise, reservation letter with initial payment, or any other document representing a commitment, or when the suspensive condition to which the disposal is subject is fulfilled At the moment of each payment or when the payment becomes due, whichever occurs first, in the disposal of real estate units resulting from real estate incorporation or land subdivision	Reference value or the disposal value of the real estate, whichever is higher, in the case of real estate disposal	Seller of the real estate, in the disposal of real estate or rights related to it

Taxable Event	Occurrence	Calculation Base	Taxpayer
Onerous act transferring or constituting real rights over real estate	At the moment of execution of the act, including any subsequent adjustments	Value of the onerous act transferring or constituting real rights over real estate	The party who establishes or transfers real rights over real estate in the onerous act constituting or transferring such rights
Lease and rental of real estate	At the moment of payment or when the payment obligation is due, whichever occurs first	Value of the lease or rental of the real estate	Lessor or lessor, in the lease or rental of real estate

Taxable Event	Occurrence	Calculation Base	Taxpayer
Real estate management and brokerage services	At the moment of service completion or payment, whichever occurs first	Value of the service provided	Provider of real estate management and brokerage services

Adjustment Reducer.

In the sale, lease, or rental of real estate by a taxpayer subject to the regular IBS and CBS regime, an amount corresponding to the adjustment reducer may be deducted from the calculation base, up to its full value.

The adjustment reducer corresponds to:

- in the case of real estate owned by the taxpayer on December 31, 2026, the reference value of the property as of that date;

- in the case of real estate acquired from January 1, 2027, from a seller not subject to the regular IBS and CBS regime, the adjustment value corresponds to the lesser of the acquisition value of the property or the reference value of the property.

In the case of leasing or renting real estate by a taxpayer under the regular IBS and CBS regime, the transaction's calculation base will be reduced each month by an amount equivalent to 1/360th of the adjustment reducer value at the time of its establishment. Upon the sale of the real estate by a taxpayer under the regular IBSand CBS regime, the calculation base will be reduced by the remaining balance of the adjustment reducer at the time of the transaction.

Social Reducer.

In the sale of new residential real estate by a taxpayer under the regular IBS and CBS regime, a social reducer of $100,000.00 (one hundred thousand [BRL]) per property may be deducted from the calculation base for IBS and CBS, up to the calculation base value, after deducting the adjustment reducer. The social reducer may be used only once for each property.

A residential property is defined as a unit built in an urban or rural area for residential purposes, according to the building regulations of the locality in which it is located and which is occupied by a person as a residence. A new property is one that has not been occupied or used, according to the regulations.

Brazilian Real Estate Registry – CIB.

Urban and rural real estate properties must be registered in the Brazilian Real Estate Registry (CIB), part of the National Land Management System (Sinter). The CIB is an inventory of urban and rural real estate properties, compiled from data submitted by originating registries. Construction projects will receive a cadastral identification in the CIB, and the IBS and CBS assessments will be conducted for each construction project.

Specific Regimes for Financial Services, Health Care Plans, and Lottery Competitions.

	Calculation Base	Rate	Forward Credit	IBS Distribution
Credit, funding and repassing, exchange, securities (TVM), securitization, and factoring	Financial service revenues (-) funding expenses (-) exchange expenses (-) losses on securities (-) financial charges on debt instruments recorded in equity (-) principal and interest losses	Maintenance of the PIS/COFINS burden on the financial sector	Yes (on financial expenses above the SELIC rate, on a cash basis, after the principal is returned and the SELIC rate is paid)	Same rule as the general regime (no identification of purchasers of each service), regulations may create a proxy for distribution
Leasing	Leasing revenue (-) funding expenses, proportional to leasing operations with non-taxpayers (-) principal and interest losses, in the same proportion	General rate (same rule as leasing and sale of goods), except for real estate, which applies the rate of the specific regime	Yes (on leasing installments and residual value actually paid, if the lessee is a taxpayer)	Same rule as the general regime (no identification of purchasers of each service), regulations may create a proxy for distribution
Consortium	All fees,	Specific	Yes (on all fees,	Impact of PL 68/2024

administration	commissions, and charges (1)	financial services rate	commissions, and charges)	Place of residence of consortium members
Insurance and reinsurance	Premiums (+) financial revenues in proportion to operations with non-taxpayers (-) indemnities paid to non-taxpayers	Specific financial services rate (2)	Yes (on the premium, if the insured is a taxpayer)	Place of residence of the insured

(1) Purchase of goods through a consortium letter of credit follows the general regime, except in the case of real estate, which follows its specific regime.
(2) Zero rate on co-insurance, retrocession, and reinsurance operations for simplification, without altering the total tax burden of the sector.

	Calculation Base	**Rate**	**Forward Credit**	**IBS Distribution**
Management and administration of resources, including investment funds	Operation value	Specific financial services rate (3)	No	Place of residence of shareholders
Payment arrangements	Portion of the MDR for each participant in the arrangement (acquirer, issuer, brand) (+) gains on the anticipation of receivables	Specific financial services rate	Yes (in the case of anticipation of receivables, same rule as for borrowers in credit operations)	Place of residence of accredited entities
Operations related to the FGTS and other public policy funds	Operation value	Rate to maintain the tax burden	No	Place of residence of shareholders (4)
Health assistance plans	Premiums (+) financial income from technical reserves (-) coverage costs with the accredited network and reimbursements	Reduced rate, corresponding to 40% of the reference rate	No	Place of residence of policyholders
Lottery contests	Bets (-) prizes (gross gaming revenue-GGR)	Reference rate	No	Place of the bets and, for online bets, place of residence of the bettors

Impact of PL 68/2024

(3) Providers of other services to the funds (e.g. accountant, auditor, lawyer) retain their respective rates.
(4) When the shareholders are exclusively government entities, the rule for government purchases applies. The same applies to the granting of credit to government entities.

Specific regimes for bars and restaurants, hospitality and parks, collective passenger transportation, SAFs, and international treaties.

	Calculation Base	Rate	Appropriation of Credits ("backward credit")	Transfer of Credits ("forward credit")
Bars and restaurants, including snack bars	Operation value of food and beverage supply, excluding tips fully passed on to employees.	Will correspond to a percentage of the standard rates of each federative entity and will be calculated to maintain the current tax burden on these operations.	Cannot appropriate credits on their purchases.	Purchasers of food and beverages supplied by bars and restaurants cannot appropriate credit.
Hospitality, Amusement Parks, and Theme Parks	Operation value for hospitality services, amusement parks, and theme parks.	Will correspond to a percentage of the standard rates of each federative entity and will be calculated to maintain the current tax burden on these operations.	Cannot appropriate credits on their purchases.	Purchasers of food and beverages supplied by bars and restaurants cannot appropriate credit
Urban, suburban, and metropolitan rail and waterway public passenger transportation	Operation value for urban, suburban, and metropolitan rail and waterway public passenger transportation services.	Rates reduced by 99%.	Cannot appropriate credits on their purchases.	Purchasers cannot appropriate credits.
Intermunicipal and interstate road, rail, and waterway public passenger transportation	Operation value for intermunicipal and interstate rail and waterway public passenger transportation services.	Will correspond to a percentage of the standard rates of each federative entity and will be calculated to maintain the current tax burden on these operations.	Can appropriate credits on their purchases	Purchasers cannot appropriate credits.

Impact of PL 68/2024

	Calculation Base	Rate	Appropriation of Credits ("backward credit")	Transfer of Credits ("forward credit")
Regional air passenger transportation	Operation value for regional air passenger transportation services.	Rates reduced by 40%.	Can partially appropriate credits on their purchases, proportional to the rate reduction	Purchasers can appropriate credits
Travel Agencies and Tourism Agencies	Sale of airline tickets by agencies: Operation value; Other intermediary services: Operation value, minus the amounts passed on to suppliers intermediated by the agency.	Sale of airline tickets by agencies: Same rate applicable to regional air transportation or other air transportation services, as the case may be. Other services: Same rate applicable to hospitality, amusement parks, and theme parks.	Can appropriate credits on their purchases as long as the amounts are not deducted from the calculation base.	Sale of airline tickets by agencies: Purchasers can appropriate credits. Other services: Purchasers cannot appropriate credits.

Impact of PL 68/2024

Selective Tax.

	Covered Products (NCM))	Calculation Base	Rates (to be defined by ordinary law)
Acquisition of Vehicles	Passenger cars and other motor vehicles primarily designed for the transport of people, including multi-purpose vehicles (8703.21.00; 8703.22.10; 8703.22.90; 8703.23.10; 8703.23.90; 8703.24.10; 8703.24.90; 8703.3; 8703.40.00; 8703.50.00; 8703.60.00; 8703.70.00; 8703.90.00); Motor vehicles for the transport of goods equipped solely with a piston engine, compression ignition (diesel or semi-diesel) or spark ignition, with a maximum load weight (gross) not exceeding 5 tons (8704.21.10; 8704.21.20; 8704.21.30; 8704.21.90; 8704.31.10; 8704.31.20; 8704.31.30; 8704.31.90); Motor vehicles for the transport of goods equipped for simultaneous propulsion with a compression ignition piston engine (diesel or semi-diesel) and an electric motor, or a spark ignition piston engine and an electric motor, with a maximum load weight (gross) not exceeding 5 tons (8704.41.00, 8704.51.00); Motor vehicles for the transport of goods equipped solely with an electric propulsion motor (8704.60.00).	Sale value during commercialization;-Auction value during auction;-Reference value in non-onerous transactions or consumption of goods (in a methodology to be defined by the head of the executive branch based on commodity and futures exchanges, orresearch agencies, or recognized and reliable government agencies); or-Book value of the asset's incorporation into fixed assets.	(1) **Ad Valorem.** For vehicles, rates may be increased or decreased depending on the following criteria: (i) vehicle power; (ii) energy efficiency; (iii) structural performance and assistive driving technologies; (iv) material recyclability; (v) carbon footprint; and (vi) technological density. Rate reduction to zero for vehicles meeting environmental sustainability criteria or purchased by people with disabilities (up to a limit of US$ 40,000), or by taxi drivers whose rights have been recognized by the Brazilian Federal Revenue (RFB). (2)

Selective Tax.

	Covered Products (NCM))	Calculation Base	Rates (to be defined by ordinary law)
Acquisition of Boats and Aircraft	Helicopters, airplanes, and other aircraft (8802), except for spacecraft (8802.60.00); Yachts and other boats and motorized recreational or sport vessels classified under NCM position 8903.	(1)	Ad Valorem. (2)
Smoking Products	Unmanufactured tobacco (2401); Cigars, cigarillos, and cigarettes (2402); Other manufactured tobacco products and substitutes; "homogenized" or "reconstituted" tobacco; tobacco extracts and sauces (2403); Products containing tobacco, reconstituted tobacco, nicotine, or tobacco or nicotine substitutes, intended for inhalation without combustion; other products containing nicotine intended for absorption into the human body (2404).		Ad Valorem and Ad Rem (NCM 2402) and only Ad Valorem (for other smoking products)
Alcoholic Beverages	Malt beers (2203); Wines (2204); Vermouths (2205); Other fermented beverages – e.g., cider, perry, mead, and sake (2206); Spirits, Whiskey, Rum, Vodka, Gin, Liqueurs, and other beverages of undenatured ethyl alcohol, with an alcohol content by volume of less than 80% volume (2208).		Ad Valorem and Ad Rem. The Ad Rem rate must consider the product of alcohol content by the volume of the package.
Sugary Beverages	Waters, including mineral and carbonated waters, with added sugar or other sweeteners or flavored (NCM 2202.10.00)		Ad Valorem.

Selective Tax.

	Covered Products (NCM))	Calculation Base	Rates (to be defined by ordinary law)
Extracted Mineral Goods	Iron ores and their concentrates, including roasted iron pyrites (2601); Crude petroleum oils (2709.00.10); Liquefied natural gas (2711.11.00); Natural gas in gaseous state (2711.21.00)		Ad Valorem, limited to 1%. For natural gas, if it is used as an input in an industrial process, the rate is reduced to 0%.

All Taxes, Contributions and Fees

ALL TAXES, CONTRIBUTIONS, AND FEES IN BRAZIL.

Before detailing the list of all taxes, contributions, and fees levied in Brazil, let's take a look at the tax burden and the approximate number of taxes (taxes, contributions, and fees) in the ten largest economies in the world. In Brazil's case, the information on the tax burden does not include the impacts expected from the Tax Reform, which could raise the percentage to approximately 35% of GDP.

1. United States
Tax burden percentage: 24.5% of GDP
Number of taxes: Approximately 30.

2. China
Tax burden percentage: 17.5% of GDP
Number of taxes: Approximately 20.

3. Japan
Tax burden percentage: 31.4% of GDP
Number of taxes: Approximately 25.

4. Germany
Tax burden percentage: 38.2% of GDP
Number of taxes: Approximately 40.

5. India
Tax burden percentage: 18.0% of GDP
Number of taxes: Approximately 25.

6. United Kingdom
Tax burden percentage: 33.5% of GDP
Number of taxes: Approximately 20.

7. France
Tax burden percentage: 45.4% of GDP
Number of taxes: Approximately 50.

8. Brazil
Tax burden percentage: 33.1% of GDP
Number of taxes: Approximately 93.

9. Italy
Tax burden percentage: 42.4% of GDP
Number of taxes: Approximately 45.

10. Canada
Tax burden percentage: 33.0% of GDP
Number of taxes: Approximately 15.

TAXES, CONTRIBUTIONS, AND FEES OF BRAZIL

0. AFRMM – Additional Freight for the Renovation of the Merchant Marine.
Purpose: To encourage the renewal and modernization of the Brazilian fleet. Application: Added to the maritime freight cost in cargo transport operations.

1. Contribution to the Directorate of Ports and Coasts (DPC).
Purpose: To fund safety and navigation regulation actions in Brazilian waters. Application: Levied on maritime transport companies.

2. Contribution to the National Horse Breeding Coordination Committee (CCCCN).
Purpose: To promote the breeding and genetic improvement of the national horse. Application: Levied on breeders and related entities.

3. Contribution to the National Fund for Scientific and Technological Development (FNDCT).
Purpose: To finance research and technological innovation projects. Application: Levied on companies benefiting from tax incentives.

4. Education Salary (FNDE).
Purpose: To finance public basic education. Application: Companies contribute at a rate of 2.5% on payroll.

5. Contribution to Funrural.
Purpose: To finance social security for rural workers. Application: Rural producers contribute a percentage of the revenue from the sale of agricultural products.

6. Contribution to INCRA.
Purpose: To promote agrarian reform and land colonization. Application: Rural businesses pay a contribution on their payroll.

7. Contribution to Work Accident Insurance (SAT/GIIL–RAT).
Purpose: To fund benefits for workers in the event of accidents.
Application: Levied on payroll with rates varying from 1% to 3%,
depending on the activity's risk.

8. Contribution to Sebrae.
Purpose: To support the development of small and micro
businesses. Application: Companies contribute 0.3% on payroll.

9. Contribution to SENAC.
Purpose: To provide vocational education for the commerce sector.
Application: Commercial enterprises contribute 1% on payroll.

10. Contribution to SENAT.
Purpose: To train workers in the transport sector. Application:
Levied on transport companies.

11. Contribution to SENAI.
Purpose: To offer vocational training for industry. Application:
Industries contribute 1% on payroll.

12. Contribution to SENAR.
Purpose: To promote education and technical assistance in the rural
sector. Application: Rural producers and agro-industries contribute
0.2% on revenue.

13. Contribution to SESI.
Purpose: To provide social and educational services to industry
workers. Application: Industrial companies contribute 1.5% on
payroll.

14. Contribution to SESC.
Purpose: To offer social and cultural services to the commerce
sector. Application: Commercial companies contribute 1.5% on
payroll.

15. Contribution to SESCOOP.
Purpose: To develop cooperatives in Brazil. Application:
Cooperatives contribute 2.5% on payroll.

16. Contribution to SEST.
Purpose: To provide health and educational services to transport
sector workers. Application: Transport companies contribute a
percentage on payroll.

17 and 18. Labor and Employer Confederative Contributions.
Purpose: To fund union entities. Application: Voluntary
contributions for employees and employers.

19. CIDE Fuels.
Purpose: To finance transport infrastructure projects. Application:
Levied on the import and sale of fuels.

20. CIDE Foreign Remittances.
Purpose: To encourage technological development in Brazil.
Application: Levied on foreign remittances related to royalties and
technical assistance.

21. Contribution for Social and Educational Assistance to
Professional Athletes (FAAP).
Purpose: To provide social benefits to athletes. Application: Levied
on athletes' salaries.

22. Contribution to Public Lighting Maintenance.
Purpose: To maintain and expand public lighting. Application:
Charged to citizens on their electricity bill.

23. CONDECINE – Contribution for the Development of the
National Film Industry.
Purpose: To promote Brazilian audiovisual production. Application:
Levied on broadcasting and telecommunications companies.

24. Contribution to Support Public Broadcasting.
Purpose: To support public radio and TV stations. Application:
Levied on broadcasting companies.

25. Social Security Contribution on Gross Revenue (CPRB).
Purpose: To replace the employer's social security contribution on
payroll, applying it to gross revenue. Application: Companies in
specific sectors can opt for this contribution method.

26 and 27. Labor and Employer Union Contributions.
Purpose: To fund union entities for employees and employers.
Application: Optional contributions after labor reform, levied on
workers and companies, respectively.

28. COFINS – Contribution for the Financing of Social Security.
Purpose: To finance social security, including health, welfare, and
social assistance. Application: Levied on companies' gross revenue,
with rates ranging from 3% (cumulative) to 7.6% (non-cumulative).

29. CBS – Contribution on Goods and Services.
Purpose: To replace COFINS and PIS/PASEP in the context of tax
reform. Application: Intended to apply to goods and services
operations, with a rate of 8.8%.

30. CSLL – Social Contribution on Net Profit.
Purpose: To finance social security. Application: Levied on
companies' net profits, with rates of 9% for most companies and
15% for financial institutions.

31. Contributions to Professional Regulatory Bodies.
Purpose: To finance professional councils, such as OAB, CRC,
CREA, among others. Application: Regulated professionals and
companies must pay annual contributions.

32. Improvement Contributions.
Purpose: To finance public works that enhance private property values, such as paving, sewage, and sidewalk improvements. Application: Charged to property owners benefiting from the value increase.

33. Aviation Fund (FAER).
Purpose: To finance the development of the aviation sector. Application: Levied on civil aviation companies.

34. Poverty Combat Fund.
Purpose: To reduce social inequalities. Application: Can be additionally levied on ICMS and other taxes.

35. State Fiscal Balance Fund (FEEF).
Purpose: To assist financially troubled states. Application: Levied on ICMS revenue, according to state law.

36. Telecommunications Supervision Fund (FISTEL).
Purpose: To supervise and regulate the telecommunications sector. Application: Levied on companies in the sector, with variable rates depending on the type of service provided.

37. Severance Indemnity Fund (FGTS).
Purpose: To protect workers dismissed without just cause. Application: Employers deposit 8% of the employee's monthly salary into a linked account.

38. Telecommunications Services Universalization Fund (FUST).
Purpose: To promote the universalization of telecommunications services. Application: Levied on companies' gross operating revenue in the sector.

39. Special Fund for Development and Improvement of Inspection Activities (Fundaf).
Purpose: To fund customs and tax inspection. Application: Levied on customs operations.

40. Funttel – Telecommunications Technological Development Fund.
Purpose: To foster technological development in the telecommunications sector. Application: Levied on companies in the sector.

41. IBS – Tax on Goods and Services.
Purpose: To replace ICMS and ISS in the context of tax reform. Application: Intended to apply to goods and services, with a state rate of 17.7%.

42. IS – Selective Tax.
Purpose: To levy on specific goods and services considered harmful to health or the environment. Application: Intended to tax products like cigarettes and alcoholic beverages.

43. ICMS – Tax on the Circulation of Goods and Services.
Purpose: The main state tax, levied on the circulation of goods and services such as transportation, telecommunications, among others. Application: Rates vary according to the state and the type of product or service.

44. Export Tax (IE).
Purpose: To regulate foreign trade and protect the national economy. Application: Levied on the export of national products.

45. Import Tax (II).
Purpose: To regulate foreign trade and protect the national industry. Application: Levied on the entry of foreign products into the country.

46. IPVA – Tax on Motor Vehicle Ownership.
Purpose: Tax on motor vehicle ownership. Application: Charged annually with rates varying from 1% to 4% depending on the state and the type of vehicle.

47. IPTU – Urban Property Tax.
Purpose: To finance municipal services. Application: Levied on urban property ownership, with rates set by municipalities.

48. ITR – Rural Property Tax.
Purpose: To regulate land use and combat rural land speculation. Application: Levied on rural properties.

49. IR – Income Tax.
Purpose: The main federal tax on income. Application: Levied on the income of individuals and companies, with progressive rates.

50. IOF – Tax on Credit, Exchange, and Insurance Transactions.
Purpose: To regulate the financial market. Application: Levied on credit, exchange, insurance, and securities transactions.

51. ITCMD – Tax on Inheritance and Donation Transfers.
Purpose: To tax the transfer of assets in the event of inheritance or donation. Application: Charged by states, with variable rates depending on the value of the transferred assets.

52. ISS – Service Tax.
Purpose: To finance municipal services. Application: Levied on the provision of services, with rates ranging from 2% to 5%, depending on the municipality and type of service.

53. PIS/PASEP – Social Integration Program and Civil Servant Asset Formation Program.
Purpose: To finance unemployment insurance and salary bonuses for workers. Application: Levied on companies' gross revenue, with rates of 0.65% (cumulative) and 1.65% (non-cumulative), and will be replaced by CBS with tax reform.

All Taxes, Contributions and Fees

54. Simples Nacional.
Purpose: To simplify taxation for micro and small businesses by unifying several taxes into a single payment. Application: Companies with annual revenues of up to BRL 4.8 million can opt for the regime, paying variable rates based on revenue and sector of activity.

55. SUDAM and SUDENE – Tax Incentives for the North and Northeast Regions.
Purpose: To promote economic development in Brazil's North and Northeast regions. Application: Companies in these regions can obtain income tax reductions or exemptions through investments in regional development activities.

56. TFF – Functioning Inspection Fee.
Purpose: To finance the inspection of business activities by municipalities. Application: Charged annually to companies operating in the municipality, with variable amounts depending on the size and type of activity.

57. TFE – Establishment Inspection Fee.
Purpose: Similar to TFF, finances the inspection of commercial and industrial establishments by the states. Application: Charged to companies based on their size and sector.

58. Public Lighting Fee (CIP or COSIP).
Purpose: To finance city lighting. Application: Charged monthly along with the electricity bill, with amounts varying according to energy consumption and municipality.

59. Garbage Collection Fee.
Purpose: To finance urban solid waste collection and disposal services. Application: Charged by municipalities, usually along with the IPTU or water bill, with amounts varying based on location and property type.

60. TUST and TUSD – Transmission and Distribution System Usage Fees.
Purpose: To cover the use of electricity transmission and distribution networks. Application: Levied on electricity bills, charged by distributors according to each customer's consumption.

61. Court Fees.
Purpose: To finance the operation of the Judiciary. Application: Charged in legal proceedings, with amounts varying depending on the type and value of the case.

62. CIDE – Economic Domain Intervention Contribution.
Purpose: To finance development programs for specific sectors such as fuels, technology, and transportation. Application: Levied on import and sale operations of petroleum, fuels, and natural gas, with variable rates depending on the product.

63. CFEM – Financial Compensation for the Exploitation of Mineral Resources.
Purpose: To compensate federal entities for the exploitation of mineral resources in their territories. Application: Levied on the gross revenue of mining companies, with rates varying depending on the type of mineral extracted.

64. Copyright and Related Rights.
Purpose: To remunerate authors, musicians, artists, and producers for the use of their works and intellectual creations. Application: Levied on the reproduction, public performance, and distribution of works protected by copyright.

65. Toll Fees.
Purpose: To finance the construction and maintenance of roads granted to the private sector. Application: Charged at toll plazas based on the type of vehicle and the length of the road traveled.

66. Fire Prevention Fee.
Purpose: To finance fire prevention and firefighting services.
Application: Charged by some states or municipalities, usually with
the IPTU or other fees, with amounts varying according to the
property and location.

67. Public Conservation and Cleaning Fee.
Purpose: To cover the maintenance of public areas, including street
and park cleaning and conservation. Application: Charged by
municipalities, typically along with the IPTU, with amounts
varying by property type.

68. TCIF – Tax on Administrative Control of Fiscal Incentives.
Purpose: To supervise tax incentives granted to companies and
ensure compliance with obligations associated with these benefits.
Application: Charged to companies receiving tax incentives, with
amounts varying according to the incentive granted.

69. TCFA – Environmental Control and Inspection Fee.
Purpose: To finance environmental inspection and control activities
that may cause environmental harm. Application: Charged annually
by IBAMA to companies engaged in potentially polluting activities,
with amounts determined by company size and environmental risk.

70. Chemical Products Control Fee.
Purpose: To control and inspect the production, marketing, and
transportation of controlled chemicals. Application: Charged to
companies dealing with controlled chemicals, with amounts
varying by activity and the quantity of products.

71. Document Issuance Fee.
Purpose: To cover the cost of issuing official documents such as ID
cards, passports, driver's licenses, among others. Application:
Charged by state or federal public agencies, with fixed or
proportional amounts based on the type of document.

72. TFAC – Civil Aviation Inspection Fee.
Purpose: To finance the inspection of civil aviation-related activities. Application: Charged by ANAC to companies in the aviation sector, such as airlines and airports, with amounts varying by activity type.

73. National Water Agency (ANA) Inspection Fee.
Purpose: To finance the inspection and control of water resource usage. Application: Charged to companies using water resources in their activities, with amounts determined by company size and water usage volume.

74. Securities Commission (CVM) Supervision Fee.
Purpose: To finance the supervision of the Brazilian capital market. Application: Charged to companies listed on the stock exchange, brokers, and other market participants, with amounts proportional to the company's size and volume of transactions.

75. Lottery, Prize, or Competition Supervision Fee.
Purpose: To control and inspect lotteries and commercial competitions. Application: Charged to companies promoting these events, with amounts varying according to the type and total value of the prizes distributed.

76. Sanitary Surveillance Inspection Fee.
Purpose: To finance sanitary inspection of products and services that affect public health. Application: Charged by ANVISA to companies in the food, pharmaceutical, cosmetics sectors, among others, with amounts proportional to the company's size and the sanitary risk of its activities.

77. Brazilian Army-Controlled Products Supervision Fee (TFPC).
Purpose: To finance the inspection and control of weapons, ammunition, explosives, and other products controlled by the Army. Application: Charged to companies manufacturing, marketing, or transporting these products, with amounts defined based on activity and product volume.

78. Private Pension Fund Inspection and Supervision Fee (TAFIC).
Purpose: To finance the supervision of closed private pension entities. Application: Charged to closed private pension entities, with amounts varying by managed assets and the number of participants.

79. Annual Vehicle Registration Fee.
Purpose: To finance the maintenance and supervision of vehicle registration. Application: Charged annually by the states, with amounts varying by the type and age of the vehicle.

80. Nuclear and Radioactive Materials Licensing, Control, and Inspection Fee.
Purpose: To finance the control and supervision of nuclear and radioactive materials usage. Application: Charged to companies handling these materials, with amounts proportional to the volume and type of activity.

81. Municipal Operating License and Permit Fee.
Purpose: To finance the inspection of economic activities at the municipal level. Application: Charged to companies for issuing an operating permit, with amounts varying by size and sector.

82. Mineral Research Fee (DNPM).
Purpose: To finance research and supervision of mining activities. Application: Charged by the National Department of Mineral Production (DNPM) to companies conducting mineral research, with amounts proportional to the explored area.

83. Manaus Free Trade Trade Zone Services Fee.
Purpose: To finance the supervision and control of activities in the Manaus Free Trade Zone. Application: Charged to companies operating in the Free Trade Zone, with amounts varying according to the type of activity.

84. Metrological Services Fee.
Purpose: To finance the verification services of measurement instruments, such as scales and taximeters. Application: Charged by INMETRO, with amounts proportional to the type of instrument and the frequency of verification.

85. Control Seal Usage Fee.
Purpose: To control the production and commercialization of products subject to special supervision, such as beverages and cigarettes. Application: Charged to companies producing these products, with amounts proportional to the production volume and the number of seals used.

86. National Petroleum Council Fees (CNP).
Purpose: To finance the regulation and supervision of petroleum activities. Application: Charged to companies operating in the exploration, refining, and distribution of petroleum, with amounts proportional to production and commercialization volume.

87. Electricity Concession and Supervision Fee.
Purpose: To finance the concession and supervision of electricity services. Application: Charged to companies holding electricity concessions, with amounts varying according to the scope and volume of energy distribution.

88. Community Radio Licensing Fee.
Purpose: To finance the concession and supervision of community radios. Application: Charged to community radio stations, with fixed amounts for the concession and renewal of licenses.

89. Terrestrial and Waterway Transportation Services Concession and Supervision Fee.
Purpose: To finance the concession and supervision of transportation services. Application: Charged to companies operating terrestrial and waterway transportation concessions, with amounts proportional to the company size and the scope of services provided.

90. Supplemental Health Fees – ANS.
Purpose: To finance the supervision of health insurance operators.
Application: Charged by ANS to health insurance operators, with
amounts proportional to the number of beneficiaries and company
size.

91. SISCOMEX Usage Fee.
Purpose: To finance the integrated foreign trade system
(SISCOMEX). Application: Charged to companies conducting
import and export operations, with amounts proportional to the
volume and type of operation.

92. Commercial Registry Fees (State Commercial Boards).
Purpose: To finance the registration of companies with the state
commercial boards. Application: Charged to companies upon their
incorporation, modification, or closure, with amounts varying based
on company size.

93. Court Fees.
Purpose: To finance the functioning of the Judiciary. Application:
Charged in legal proceedings, with amounts proportional to the
value of the case and the type of process.

94. Administrative Council for Economic Defense (CADE) Process
Fees.
Purpose: To finance CADE's activities in controlling and
suppressing anticompetitive practices. Application: Charged in
administrative proceedings involving mergers, acquisitions, and
practices of economic defense, with amounts proportional to the
size of the companies involved and the economic impact of the
operation.

INDEX OF PL 68/2024

FINAL TEXT FROM THE CHAMBER OF DEPUTIES
link:
https://legis.senado.leg.br/sdleg-getter/documento?
dm=9725946&ts=1725410367618&disposition=inline

PROCEEDINGS IN THE FEDERAL SENATE
link:
https://www25.senado.leg.br/web/atividade/materias/-/ma
teria/164914#tramitacao_10875162

Index of PL 68/2024

ANNEX XXI
(Law No. 123, of December 14, 2006)

ANNEX IV
Rates and Allocation of the Simples Nacional for
Revenues from the Provision of Services Listed in § 5º-C
of Art. 18 of this Complementary Law

ANNEX XXII
(Law No. 123, of December 14, 2006)

ANNEX V
Rates and Allocation of the Simples Nacional for
Revenues from the Provision of Services Listed in § 5º-I
of Art. 18 of this Complementary Law

ANNEX XXIII
(Law No. 123, of December 14, 2006)

ANNEX VII
Fixed Values of the Individual Microentrepreneur (MEI)

Here is the continuation of the translation:

ANNEX XXIV
(Law No. 123, of December 14, 2006)

ANNEX VI
Rates and Allocation of the Simples Nacional for
Revenues from the Provision of Services Related to
Logistics, Transportation, and Storage

THE TAX REFORM CALCULATOR.

I created the calculator as a tool with the purpose of offering the reader a way to compare the current tax system with the VAT.

The calculator can be accessed on my website heronrobledo.com. There, you will find a link to load the calculator. If you prefer, you can use the QR-Code below:

To prevent misuse, it is necessary to provide an access code. This code, in turn, is available on the pages of this book.

The calculator is available in Portuguese, English, and Spanish.

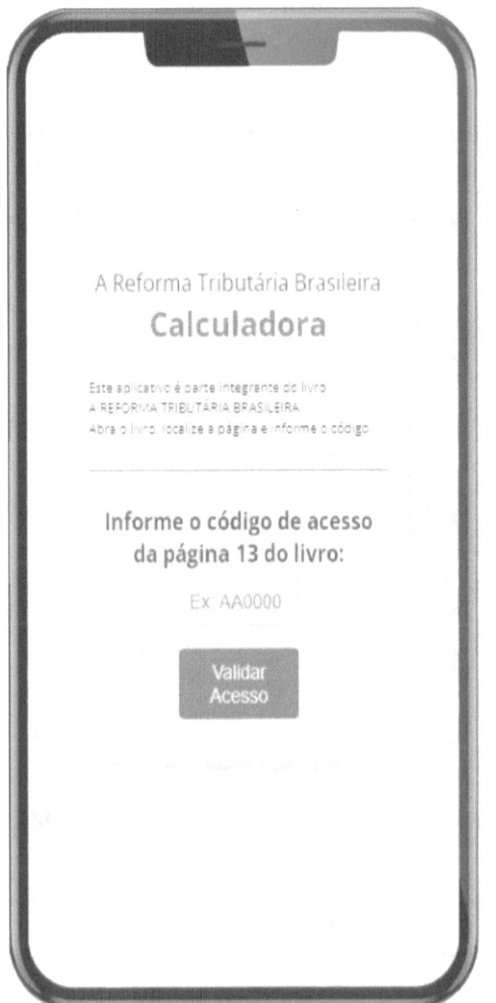

Figure 3.

Access to the Calculator.

Figure 3 shows the access interface to the calculator.

Enter the access code as requested. In this example, the application asks you to provide the code found on page 13 of this book.

Click the "Validate Access" button to proceed.

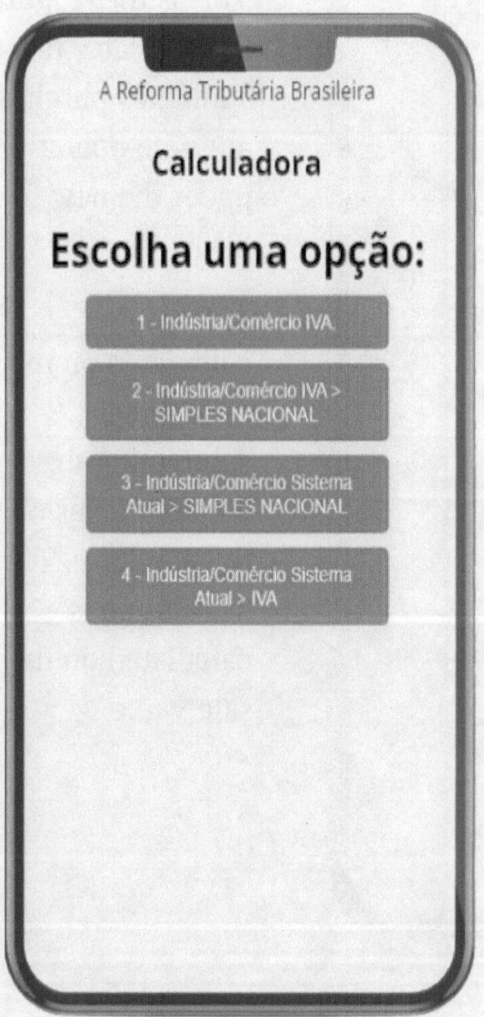

Figure 4.

The Calculator Control Panel

The Control Panel of the calculator (Figure 4) displays 4 buttons with options for the available contexts in the calculator.

Choose one of them to proceed.

Figure 5.

This is the (Figure 5) calculator that simulates purchase and sale operations under the new VAT.

The tax is calculated on the difference, subtracting the credited taxes on the purchase. The tax burden is calculated on the sale value.

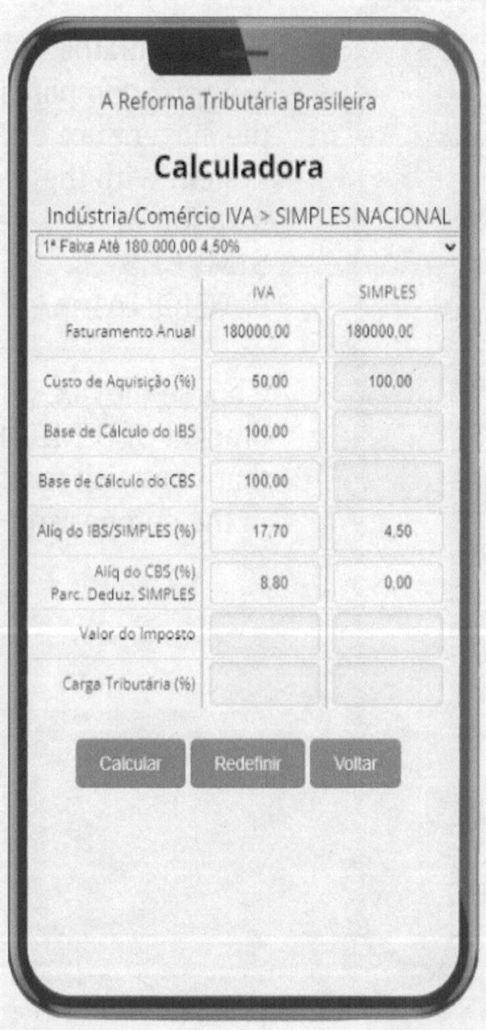

Figure 6.

The purpose of this calculator (Figure 6) is to provide a comparison between VAT taxation and SIMPLES NACIONAL.

Remember that SIMPLES neither appropriates nor grants the right to tax credits.

Choose from the list the tax bracket of SIMPLES that you want to use in the comparison.

	SISTEMA ATUAL	SIMPLES
Faturamento Anual	180000,00	180000,00
Custo de Aquisição (%)	50,00	50,00
Base de Cálculo do ICMS	100,00	
Base de Cálculo do IPI	100,00	
Aliq do ICMS/SIMPLES (%)	18,00	4,50
Aliq do IPI (%) Parc. Deduz. SIMPLES	10,00	0,00
PIS/COFINS (%)	3,65	
Valor do Imposto		
Carga Tributária (%)		

Figure 7.

The calculator in Figure 7 compares the current tax system with the taxation of SIMPLES NACIONAL.

Choose the tax bracket of SIMPLES that you wish to use in the comparison.

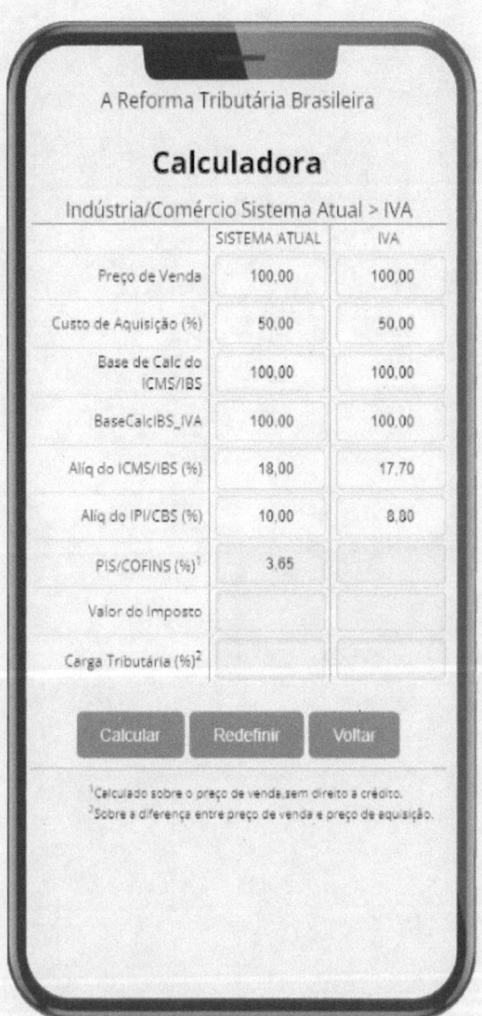

	SISTEMA ATUAL	IVA
Preço de Venda	100,00	100,00
Custo de Aquisição (%)	50,00	50,00
Base de Calc do ICMS/IBS	100,00	100,00
BaseCalcIBS_IVA	100,00	100,00
Alíq do ICMS/IBS (%)	18,00	17,70
Alíq do IPI/CBS (%)	10,00	8,80
PIS/COFINS (%)[1]	3,65	
Valor do Imposto		
Carga Tributária (%)[2]		

Figure 8.

And finally, this calculator (Figure 8) compares the current tax system with the IVA.

Since the logic of the calculators allows for editable tax bases and rates, it can be used to simulate any taxes, including those on services.

From the Author.

Motivated by my five decades of experience in the business world and the need to understand the complexities of the Brazilian tax reform, I wrote this guide. With over 30 years of experience developing systems for companies across various sectors, I have had the opportunity to closely witness the challenges posed by the Brazilian tax system.

I believe that my unique perspective, combined with deep technical knowledge, can help businesses, developers, accountants, and public agents navigate the changes and optimize their processes.

This book aims to provide a comparative analysis between the current tax system and the proposed reform, helping readers understand the implications of the new rules and make more informed decisions. Throughout the work, I present practical and comparative examples to facilitate the understanding of the concepts and aid in adapting to the new requirements.

I hope this guide is useful to all those who wish to delve deeper into the topic of Brazilian tax reform.

Heron Robledo.

AUTHOR'S WORKS.

My works, some in more than one language, can be found at the following electronic addresses:

heronrobledo.com

In the following marketplaces, search for "heron robledo":

amazon.com
amazon.com.br
loja.uiclap.com.br
clubedeautores.com.br
draft2digital.com

Books:

Some of the books have versions in Portuguese, English and Spanish.

Translations:

Gospel – New Vulgate Vaticana.
Gospel of Mary.
Childhood Gospel of Jesus.
Gospel of John – Vulgate.

The History of the Church – The Primitive Church.
True Stories of Lost Navigators.

Study:

101 Questions for God.
Spiritism according to the Gospel.

Humor:

TREATISE ON UFOLOGY AND CALLIGRAPHY. A humorous joke with the people who explore flying saucers and abductions but never prove it.

MANIFESTO HETERO. A healthy joke with the LGBT people.

Realistic Fantasy:

THE RESCUE OF THE EARTH.
An adventure about the recreation of the Earth carried out by Special Children whose promised ones are soul mates. The Earth is rebuilt on Mount Roraima with the help of Cyclopes.
Dragons and nice aliens complete the story.

THE MACHINE DECIDES.
An artificial intelligence takes over the mind and body of a 25-year-old girl and turns her into the most beautiful and powerful woman on Earth.

THE CIA AND THE COUP OF 64 IN BRAZIL.
A humorous parody of this part of Brazilian history.
John Turner-a bumbling but charming CIA agent-carries out the seizure of power by fomenting coup plotters and anti-coup plotters.

ARIMATHEA ORATORIUM.

In an unexpected spiritualist section, Joseph of Arimathea tells unpublished stories about Jesus and the Holy Grail.

THE PRACTICAL COURSE OF AN INVESTIGATIVE MYTHOLOGIST.

An adventure for five young people in São Tomé das Letras.

In the story, the fairy Angela guides the girls to Machu-Pichu, where a Disney show is mixed with a Taylor Swfit concert.